DUROBRIVAE

A ROMAN TOWN BETWEEN FEN AND UPLAND

DUROBRIVAE

A ROMAN TOWN BETWEEN FEN AND UPLAND

GARRICK FINCHAM

TEMPUS

To Gill, for being there

First published 2004

Tempus Publishing Ltd
The Mill, Brimscombe Port
Stroud, Gloucestershire GL5 2QG
www.tempus-publishing.com

British Library Cataloguing in Publication Data.
A catalogue record for this book is available from the British Library.

ISBN 0 7524 3337 7

Typesetting and origination by Tempus Publishing.
Printed and bound in Great Britain.

CONTENTS

ACKNOWLEDGEMENTS

I would like to thank the many people that have given me assistance during the writing of this book, particularly Gillian Hawkes and Theo Weiner for their input. I would also like to thank Julia Habeshaw and Ben Robinson of Peterborough Museum and Art Gallery and Roger Kipling, Richard Buckley and Nick Cooper of ULAS for their help in sourcing illustrations. I would also like to thank Melanie Cameron and Gillian Hawkes for their drawings and photographs that do so much to enliven my text. Much thanks must also go to the staff at Tempus, for all their hard work – without them this book would not have been possible.

All illustrations and photographs are by the author, unless otherwise stated.

1

WHY DUROBRIVAE?

This is a book about the Roman town of Durobrivae, the urban centre of which lies close to modern-day Peterborough *(1)*. However, when we use the word 'town' we need to start by being clear about what we think it means. Of course we mean the buildings and structures of the urban centre itself, those are important, but towns are also much more than that. A good example of what this means, though it is only one, is food supply. People who live in towns in any period rarely, if ever, produce enough food to support themselves. Almost by definition a town, as a more or less densely occupied and built-up area, relies upon food (and much else) that is produced elsewhere. Some of what a town relies upon will be brought from a great distance – what we broadly term imports. In the Roman period in Britain this might be, for example, amphorae (large pottery containers mostly used for the transport of liquid goods) containing olive oil that came from Spain, or fine ware pottery that was manufactured in Gaul. However, in the ancient world it was expensive to transport staple goods long distances, and most of the things that a town required to survive – pottery, food, or metal work, for example – had to be produced locally. A Roman town, therefore, lay at the centre of a network of relationships that stretched out into the countryside around, and way beyond, and it was these relationships that allowed it to fulfil its needs. Such relationships were, of course, two way, with the town providing services for the landscape around it, like a market, administration, and perhaps justice. So we can see that, when considering a town, to ignore what we call the 'hinterland', is to consider only a small part of a vast working whole, and that alone cannot possibly allow us to explain how that town worked, how it was supported, and what effect it had upon the rural landscape beyond the walls and suburbs. This is a book not only about a town, but a whole town: everything that went to make it work, all the farmers and craftsmen who drove or hauled what they had to sell to the urban centre for market day, and consequently we shall be thinking more about the countryside than the town itself. The first theme

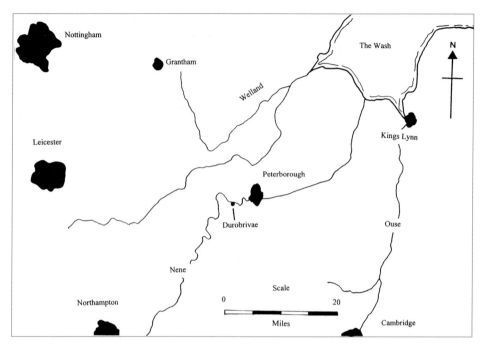

1 The site of the Roman town of Durobrivae in relation to the modern landscape

of this book, then, is to consider the working whole of a Roman town, and thus to create a picture of how one may have functioned.

This leads us on to a consideration that underlies the approach taken in this book, which is about 'perception'. It is important, if we are to understand past landscapes, to try and think about what is left (in this case the archaeology of Roman Britain) in terms that would have made sense to the people we are studying, rather than simply in ways that are convenient for modern scholars. Many studies of past landscapes use modern boundaries to establish the extent of their study area. Such an approach might take the form of studying the Roman period in a particular county, or parish *(2)*. However, viewing the landscape in this way distorts how we perceive the past. A county, the boundaries of which are relevant to the modern organisation of Britain, may cut across Roman social divisions. If the territory of a Roman town happens to straddle a county boundary, a country-based study will see only half the picture. The approach taken here is to ask: what was the extent of the territory of the Roman town that we are studying? The answer to that question forms the basis for the area we will look at – again, the aim is to establish the nature of a working whole, and then to attempt to understand the landscape from the perspective of those who inhabited it.

The theme of perception can be taken further. We are in the habit, when studying a landscape, to think in terms of maps and plans. However, this is not the way in which the landscape in the past will have been experienced. There were maps in the ancient world, perhaps the most notable being the *Forma Urbis,* a map of the city of Rome carved on marble and dating to the reign of Septimius Severus (193-211), or the cadasters, essentially surveys to record who owned what to facilitate taxation. But the most widespread kind of map, and probably the type which would have been most familiar and comprehensible to citizens of the empire, was the itinerary *(3).* This kind of map, as the name implies, was more a recorded journey than a 'map', noting stopping places and destinations, and often distances. The most famous example is the Antonine Itinerary, covering most of the empire, including Britain, and giving a rather 'schematic' understanding of places, and the roads that connected them. If the very tool that we use so often to understand a landscape, the traditional 'aerial view' map, would have been largely alien to the Roman mind, it cannot give us any kind of sense of how the landscape was perceived, nor how the territory that we are trying to study was understood. The map, however, is a tool that we understand, and its use is essential to comprehending Durobrivae and its hinterland, but we shall also look at the landscape in a way inspired more by the itinerary, in an attempt to give us a 'Roman' perspective.

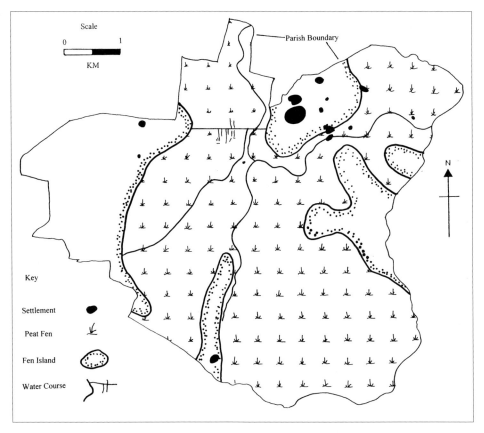

2 Example of the kind of information provided by archaeological survey. This example shows a parish map, like that produced by the Fenland Survey during the 1980s and 1990s. *After Hall, 1987*

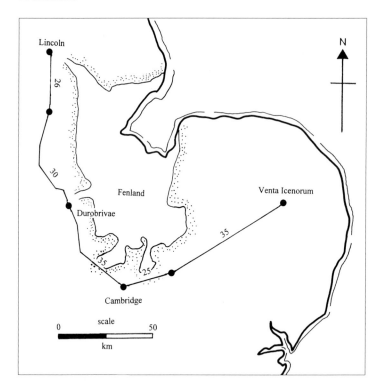

3 Illustration of an Itinerary Map. This section, which covers the roads around Durobrivae, is taken from the Antonine Itinerary, with distances shown in Roman miles. *After Dilke, 1985*

A third aspect of perception is the passage of time. When considering the Roman landscape, we tend to think of the developed Roman period, say the second century. Anything that is before this is the evolution of Roman Britain, anything much after is its decline. When mapping the Roman features of an area this leads us into producing one map – the 'full' Roman picture. The truth about the way the landscape will have felt to those who lived in it is that it will have evolved, changed over time, with one phase of development flowing into the next. The effort is made here to produce multiple maps of different periods, and multiple explanations of how the area under consideration worked at different times of its history under Roman control. The town and hinterland of Durobrivae was not a static place, as we shall see.

If these issues are the key themes of this book, why is Durobrivae a good case study through which to consider them? The town has not been studied in a systematic way before, but it is one of the largest, and most interesting of what have been termed the 'small towns'. Large towns in the Roman Britain had distinct legal identity, fitting into one of several categories, and the occasional attempt has been made to claim that Durobrivae had a specific legal status. However, below these were urban settlements, sometimes of some size, but with no official rank, and usually unplanned: what we term small towns. Durobrivae is usually considered to belong to this second group of settlements, but unusual amongst these because it is of its comparatively large size, being almost a small city;

it has an extensive walled area at its heart and also has a concentration of industry centred upon it. This offers us opportunities.

A principal problem with investigating Durobrivae, as we shall see in Chapter Two, is the very small amount of excavation done within the confines of the defences surrounding the core of the urban settlement. Consequently, we know little in any detail about this area, arguably the most important part of the town, as it contains the main public buildings. However, we have a very good overall idea of the plan of the town, and we know enough to form at least a broad understanding of the history of the settlement's development. This lack of precise knowledge might actually be seen as a benefit to a study like this one – if we knew much more about this central area, our thoughts would necessarily be concentrated there, to the detriment of wider issues. As it is, we have to make do with a thumbnail sketch of the town itself, and look further afield in any attempt to understand the broader story of Durobrivae.

Here, we are well served. To consider the town as a working whole, we must also have some evidence of what was going on in that hinterland, and Durobrivae is particularly rich in this respect. The town sat at the heart of a complex landscape in which not only agriculture, but also a range of what we might loosely term 'industrial' activities were pursued. We will define the hinterland of Durobrivae in a moment, but for now it is sufficient to note that it includes the salt-making activities of the inhabitants of the Fenland, both to the east in the Central Fens around the small modern town of March, and to the north-east on the wide expanses of the Lincolnshire Silt Fens *(4)*. It includes the Nene Valley potteries to the west, and, further up the river valley, substantial iron workings associated with the East

4 The typical flat landscape of the Fens, to the east of Durobrivae. Note the drainage ditch in the foreground

5 Typical rolling landscape to the west of Durobrivae. Contrast this with the Fenland landscape in *(4)*

Midlands ore fields *(5)*. There was also a possible mosaic school based upon the town in the later Roman period. Most of the inhabitants of the area were probably still predominantly farmers, but the industries listed above are important, because they leave readily identifiable traces in the archaeological record. We should not let the visibility of such traces blind us to the fact that they are only part of the story, and that alongside salt production, pottery and the rest the land was being tilled and livestock reared. However, such industrial activity can act as an important indicator of the levels of economic activity over and above basic survival, give clues to the economic organisation of the area, and indicate the possibility of important links to the institutions of the wider empire.

For the Fens particularly we are also lucky enough to have a wealth of survey information. An archaeological survey involves walking across the landscape collecting any visible sign of past occupation, and typical finds might include building material (bricks and tiles) and/or pottery *(6)*. This often provides little more than an indication that a site was present, and perhaps a crude idea of the date of that site, but it is information that can be collected across a wide area relatively quickly and cheaply when compared to full-scale excavation. The breadth of this information compensates for its lack of detail, and allows us to reconstruct, at least in superficial terms, the way that the landscape worked.

So the large quantities of information available, the identifiable industries, and the fact that we have a thumbnail sketch of the history of the town, are all factors that combine to make Durobrivae a uniquely apt focal point when considering how a town functioned in the context of the wider landscape.

ULAS Fieldwalking Record Sheet	Site Accession no:	

Site Name:	Parish:	County:
OS Field name/No:	ULAS Field No:	Nat Grid Square: ,

	Name:	Address:	Phone:
Landowner:			
Tenant:			

Date walked:	Photo Nos:
Purpose:	Method:
Distance of lines	Approximate direction: N-S / E-W / NE-SW / NW-SE

CONDITIONS am / pm

Visibility: Good / Indifferent / Poor   **Cloud cover:** Continuous / Broken / None

Sun : even light / high sunlight with little shadow / low sunlight with strong shadow

GROUND CONDITIONS

State of Land: a) Wet / Damp / Dry / Frozen

b) Ploughed and unweathered / ploughed and weathered / sown /

If sown, was crop

c) Not yet through / just through / thick but viable for walking /

Are there signs that ploughing has cut into the subsoil? Yes / No / Unclear

As follows:

Geology:	Description of ploughsoil:
Fieldwalking team:	
EDM Files:	Finds Codes:

Notes/Sketch of transects and topography:

Recorded by:	Date	Checked

6 Recording sheet for field walking. Using such recording sheets we can collect information that, although often lacking in detail, has great breadth, as it can cover large geographical areas. This example is the sheet used by the University of Leicester Archaeological Service, and is reproduced with their permission

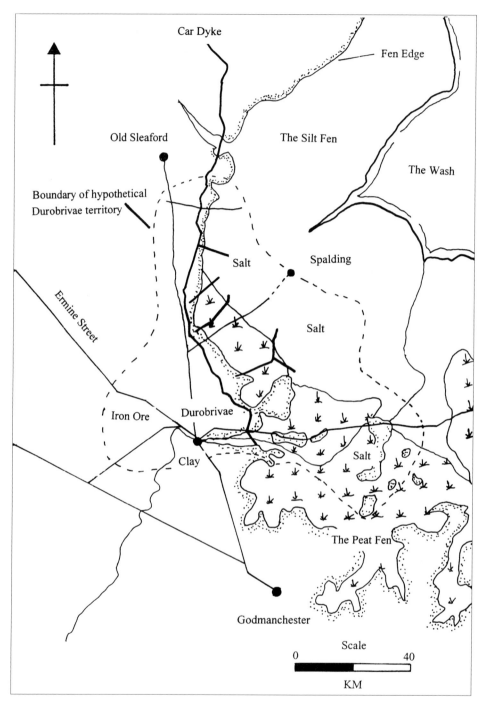

Car Dyke

Fen Edge

Old Sleaford

The Silt Fen

The Wash

Boundary of hypothetical
Durobrivae territory

Salt

Spalding

Ermine Street

Salt

Iron Ore

Durobrivae

Salt

Clay

The Peat Fen

Godmanchester

Scale

0   40

KM

7 A map of the hypothesised territory of the town of Durobrivae, showing principal roads and resources

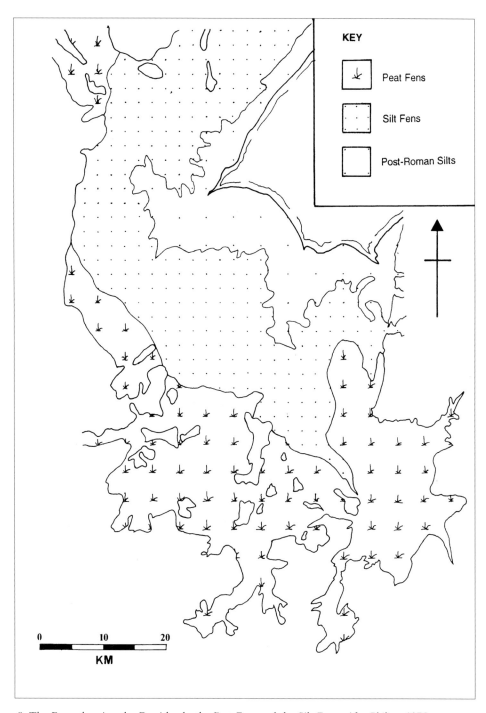

KEY

Peat Fens

Silt Fens

Post-Roman Silts

0   10   20
KM

8 The Fens, showing the Fen islands, the Peat Fens and the Silt Fens. *After Philips, 1970*

But how do we know what the hinterland of the town actually was? If we are going to consider the town in a way that would have made sense to its inhabitants, we must establish which parts of the surrounding countryside were associated with Durobrivae. In short, we must define the town's territory. This is not a particularly easy task as there are no literary sources that may be of help, and attempting to re-establish political or administrative boundaries from archaeology is notoriously difficult. Without specific evidence like the 'boundary stones' found in some parts of the empire like North Africa that indicate the divisions between the territories of coastal towns like Lepcis Magna, Oea or Sabratha, there is no direct way of understanding where those territorial boundaries lay.

The answer to this puzzle lies in the effect that political factors had in shaping the 'social' landscape that developed in the region during the Roman occupation. By this we mean the combination of local communications (rivers and roads), the distribution of settlements and industries, what products were produced within the territorium of the town, what the distribution of those products can tell us about the organisation of that territory, and the connections that territory had with other places. When combined with other clues that the archaeological data can give us, we can establish the approximate boundaries of a possible territory *(7)*. To understand how these boundaries were arrived at we must start to the east of the town, in the flat lands of the Fens.

The area to the east of the town, the Fens *(8)*, has traditionally been considered as an imperial estate, and so not properly part of the town. As we shall see in Chapters Three and Four, the concept of large, monolithic land holdings, owned by the imperial household, or, indeed, anyone else, now appears unlikely. So if the area was not an imperial estate, and was a part of the ordinary 'civil' landscape of the region, how and why did it relate to the town? If we examine the road system connecting the town to the Fens we see two interesting things. Firstly, the layout of local communications in this area illustrates the likelihood that Durobrivae was the principal urban centre serving the Fens. The road connections between the uplands and the Silt Fens of Lincolnshire and northern Cambridgeshire are arranged in a highly significant way. King Street is the road that runs north out of the town, skirts the western edge of the Fens and finally reaches Sleaford. However, periodic roads run out from it, east into the Fens. The Car Dyke, a Roman earthwork also running along the western edge of the Fens and which may, amongst other things, have been a canal, also follows roughly the same route, and spur canals jut out from it into the Fens in a similar manner to the roads. This means that, for inhabitants of the Fens, contact with the nearest major urban centre was via this Fen Edge road, or the Car Dyke. One other site that has been advanced as a possible centre for the Fens, the settlement of Stonea, in the Central Fen area, has no communications connecting it with most of the Silt Fens at all, and so cannot have administered this area. Thus either Durobrivae or Old Sleaford must have acted as the administrative centre for the salt industry which developed out on the Fens, the 'market centre' for the salt producers. As Old Sleaford never grew into a major town during the Roman period, this makes Durobrivae the natural candidate as this urban focus.

Secondly, the Central Fens are accessible by only one road – the Fen Causeway. This road ultimately connects Durobrivae to the territory of the Iceni to the east, but Durobrivae is the closest urban settlement to the Central Fen territories. There are also several other factors that point to a close association between the Central Fens and the town. The pottery used there in the Roman period is definitely that of the west, not that used to the east, inferring that these settlements traded most in that direction. The other factor is that this area, like that of the Silt Fens, supported a salt production industry, and if it is the case that the town acted as the market centre for salt production in one area of the Fens with which it had strong road links, the same is also probably the case for the Central Fens. So, as with the Silt Fen sites, the logical urban centre for the Central Fen industries is Durobrivae. Thus, based upon the communications of the region, we may strongly suggest that settlements of the Silt and Central Fens were within the wide economic hinterland of Durobrivae. But what of the west, on the uplands?

To the immediate west of the town, and further up the Nene Valley, lies a concentration of villas, the large rural establishments of the wealthy. Owners of these houses were of the class that would have taken a leading role in the running of the town – the class that will have supplied members of the town's ruling council. These villas should certainly, then, be seen as apart of the social and economic whole of which the town formed the heart. But clustered along the Nene Valley, amongst the areas occupied by the villas, we also find kilns of the Nene Valley pottery industry. The exact relationship between villas, kilns and the town we will explore later, but, as with the salt industry, Durobrivae forms the logical urban centre through which products of the industry would have been traded. The distribution of this pottery is, in fact, a concrete link between the Nene, the town and the Fens.

There is another industry in the region which might also have had significance for Durobrivae: iron production. There is evidence from the suburbs of the town of iron working, and this activity connects the town to the East Midlands ore fields. The presence of this iron-working activity in the town itself suggests that any territory we are looking to define should also include ore fields, and that the hinterland of the town was wide. Whilst these boundaries can only ever be approximate, and are of course deductions, and thus open to challenge, they nonetheless form the basis of a possible reconstruction of the town's economic territory.

Having set the boundaries for the breadth of our study, we should next look at the history of archaeological research in the area. As mentioned above, the amount of actual fieldwork within Durobrivae itself is surprisingly small. The principal excavator (although we do have other sources of information besides excavation) is still Edmund Artis, a nineteenth-century antiquary, who worked for his patron, Earl Fitzwilliam. Artis conducted a series of excavations throughout the area,

9 An example of the plates produced by Edmund Artis in the early nineteenth century, showing excavations of the villa beneath the village of Castor. Although these plates provide us with a large amount of information, no accompanying text was ever produced. *Reproduced courtesy of Peterborough Museum and Art Gallery*

including some on the town itself, where he identified some significant buildings in the urban centre, and others under the village of Castor to the north. Artis' investigations revealed the existence of Roman buildings of some substance, but the location of many is still uncertain. A volume of illustrations, entitled *The Durobrivae of Antoninus*, gives us much information about his discoveries, but the companion volume of explanatory text was never published *(9)*.

In the twentieth century, excavation has been conducted on the 'suburbs' of the town, that is to say the areas which lie outside the walled area at the heart of Durobrivae. This shift of interest was encouraged by the fact that the core of the town is now a scheduled monument, severely restricting any possible archaeological investigation that might be conducted there. The southern suburb was investigated in the mid-1950s, excavations which revealed extensive extra-mural settlement lined along a road running around the south-western edge of the defences. To the north there were excavations in Normangate Field and at Kate's Cabin, particularly during the late 1960s and early to mid-1970s, where there was evidence of industrial activity including iron working and pottery production, as well as occupation.

All of this excavation, however, has been on a small scale, and can provide us with only fragmentary information about the town. The most useful information that we possess comes from aerial photography, and the Nene Valley Research Committee has produced a fine composite plan of the town and its environs, made

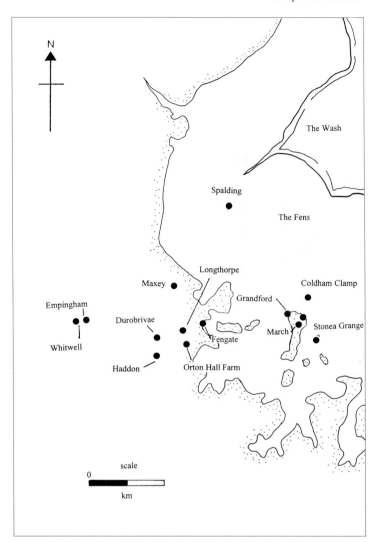

10 Map showing the principal excavations within the proposed hinterland of Durobrivae

up of many crop marks seen on a variety of photographs (see the 'Taking Your Interest Further' section at the end of this book for details of material in print that covers most aspects of the town and its hinterland in more detail than possible here). This gives us an excellent idea of the overall layout of the town, if not a particularly clear idea of how it developed over time.

Turning to the territory beyond the town, in the east we have the Fens, and the two great surveys, *Fenland in Roman Times*, and the *Fen Survey*. These surveys give us a great deal of information about the overall layout of the landscape, albeit without the detail which excavation would provide. They also identify the locations of salterns, sites where salt was produced by evaporation, allowing us to get a good idea of the scale and physical extent of the industry. A recent study by Fincham has analysed this data on settlement and industry, and provided a detailed model of the development of the area, a model which will be used as our starting point in Chapters Three and Four. The Fens have seen some excavation, particularly in the Central Fen area, principally conducted by the late Dr Tim Potter. Especially important are the excavations, under the direction of Jackson and Potter, by the British Museum at the site of Stonea Grange. This was a major settlement, at the heart of which was a large tower-like structure which would have dominated this area of the Fenland. Other excavations, though on a much smaller scale, have been conducted across the region, like that at Coldham Clamp (also by Tim Potter), and various small investigations by commercial archaeological units, often on archaeology facing destruction by development. These 'grey' reports are not usually fully published, and are often on such a small scale that, although they are useful to provide illustrations of different types of site, they rarely provide sufficient detail to be truly informative.

Off the Fens, we have more excavation evidence *(10)*. This comes from sites on or near the Fen Edge, like Fengate, excavated by Francis Pryor; or Orton Hall Farm, excavated by Don Mackreth under the auspices of the Nene Valley Excavation Committee. These excavated sites, east of the urban centre but on the upland, or the very edge of the Fen, probably give us our best indications of the kind of settlement to be found in western parts of Durobrivae's hinterland.

To the west we also have numerous investigations of kilns of the Nene Valley pottery industry. There have been several key studies of the pottery industry, principally *Roman Pottery from the Nene Valley: A Guide*, published by Peterborough Museum which gives an indication of the types of pottery produced and their dates, and V. Swann's study *Pottery Kilns of Roman Britain* contains a substantial section on the Nene Valley. Recent work has also been done on the East Midlands' iron-smelting industry. This has been principally conducted by Irene Shrüffer-Kolb, and much of it is unpublished. However, it does give us a chance to understand the iron industry in the region in more detail than has previously been the case. Finally, of course, we have the villas of the region. In common with much of the archaeology to the west of the town, we have an idea of where these structures are located, but there are no up-to-date excavations to give us a detailed insight. Knowledge of how the villas are distributed through the landscape, however, will at least allow us to relate them to other aspects of the town.

Thus we can see that the area identified as Durobrivae's hinterland provides us with a wealth of evidence of various kinds. This evidence, when considered as part of a functioning social and economic landscape, can allow us to examine the wider context of an urban centre, and can go a long way towards compensating for our lack of excavation in the town itself. However, before we begin to consider how that evidence fits together to give a picture of the life around the town, we will consider in detail what we know about Durobrivae itself.

2

A BRIEF HISTORY
OF THE TOWN

Although, as pointed out in Chapter One, there is little in the way of modern excavated evidence from Durobrivae, the fact that we have a substantially complete plan of the town is, perhaps, surprising. This is thanks to the work of the Nene Valley Excavation Committee, which, using aerial photographs, has provided us with a street map of the complex layout of the urban centre. This shows not the planned layout of some Roman towns like Verulamium or Corinium Dobunnorum, but an irregular jumble of streets (*11* and *12*). It is possible, even from just such a plan, to get an idea of Durobrivae's history; however, because of the kind of evidence that we are using, this is not a detailed picture, but a thumbnail sketch. But even such a sketch allows us to move towards understanding the town and its link to the wider landscape.

It seems clear that there was no Iron Age predecessor to the town – the landscape around the Nene Crossing in the pre-Roman period was one of small farmsteads, located in a close network of fields. If the area around the excavated site of Orton Hall Farm is any indication, these farms might have consisted of small clusters of buildings and enclosures, linked together over considerable distances by drove ways. These droves may also have acted as boundaries in the landscape, separating arable land from areas of grazing. The nearest major centre at this period would have been Old Sleaford, which, as we shall see later, acted as the market centre for small settlements located on the edge of the Fens. The populations of such Fen Edge sites may have gone out into the marshes in the summer months to hunt, fish, and produce salt. Any produce acquired for trade may well have been sold on through the market at Sleaford. One such Fen Edge site would have been Fengate, an extensive complex of buildings and enclosures now covered by the light industry of eastern Peterborough.

The Roman army penetrated the area in AD 47, and were quick to establish control of the crossing over the River Nene – a small fort, to the south of the river, is visible on the aerial photographs (*12*). Although no excavation has been conducted upon this site, it was clearly positioned in a way which commands the

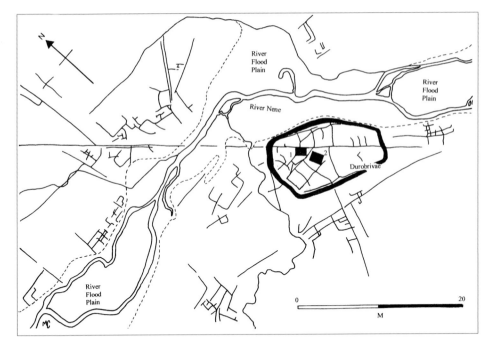

11 A plan of the principal crop marks in the immediate area of Durobrivae. The plan shows the walled area of the town an the site of the possible *mansio* (1) and *forum* (2). This plan is based closely upon the work of the Nene Valley Research Committee. *After Macketh, 1995*

12 Looking towards the site of the first-century fort

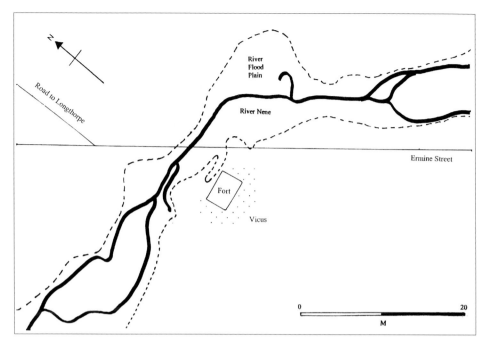

13 Early settlement – the fort and *vicus*

roads laid out in the first century. We should also note that upon other military sites in the region occupation was invariably of first-century date. Both of these facts combined are enough to strongly suggest that the installation by the Nene should be dated to that period. That being the case, it was almost certainly a satellite of the fortress at Longthorpe, approximately two miles to the east, and also located on the Nene (though this time to the north of the river). Indeed, Longthorpe, being a large military installation with satellite forts (there is also a fort of the first century at Grandford as well as a possible sequence of forts at Eldernell, both sites located in the Fens), was probably the focus of Roman power and a military administration for the area following the Conquest.

The satellite fort's location guarding the Nene Crossing *(12)*, however, might have been decisive in sparking the development of an urban centre here. The fort, lying at the junction of a major inland waterway, the Nene, and a major north–south route, Ermine Street, was clearly in a key site for controlling local movement, and thus trade. The presence of soldiers at this location would also have encouraged people with things to sell, and services to offer (so-called camp followers) to gather there. At many military establishments like, for example, Housesteads on Hadrian's Wall, this situation led to the growth of a civilian settlement around the fort – termed a *vicus*. We see elements of a possible *vicus* around the Nene Valley Fort, preserved in the crop marks. Several streets are visible outside the defences, and these streets, though dating to a later time, may perpetuate the original *vicus* streets *(13)*.

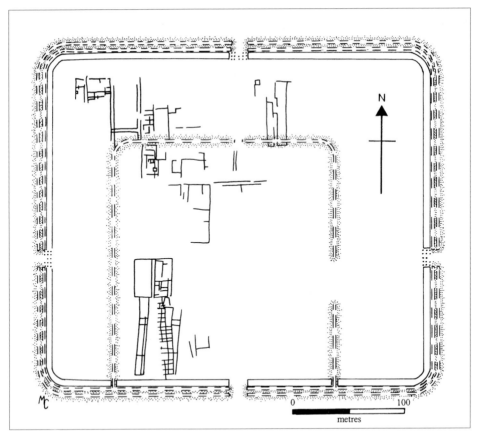

14 Plan of the Roman fortress at Longthorpe. Note the outline of the smaller, later fort, within the earlier fortress. *After St Joseph, 1974. Illustration by Melanie Cameron*

The military presence in this area came to an end sometime before AD 100. The main fortress at Longthorpe was abandoned early in the second half of the first century, though a second fort, of much reduced size, was constructed on the same site *(14)*. There is no evidence, however, that this smaller fort lasted beyond the end of the first century. The satellite forts in the Fens also appear to have been abandoned at a similar time, suggesting that the whole military occupation of the area came to an end as the army moved on to complete the conquest of the north. However, this is probably not quite the complete picture.

The problem, in respect of the military occupation and control of the area in the years following the Conquest, is what happened in the area after the army had moved on, but before the town developed? This is a difficult question to answer, and we have no evidence that bears directly upon it. But a possible solution is that a small military staff governed and organised the area. The principal installations, no longer needed, were abandoned as the bulk of the army was moved on, leaving behind a form of 'skeleton' military administration. This small staff would leave no direct traces in the archaeology, and it is difficult to prove that they existed. But the area would need to be administered somehow, and when the army departed it was clearly not developed enough to form its own civilian administration. The military staff, assisting in transition to a more settled form of government, seem the most likely possibility, as they might also have exercised responsibility for securing supplies for the army. As is argued later, the huge growth of industry around Durobrivae is probably explained by enduring links with the army and its supply chain. It is perhaps during this slightly ambiguous phase of the Roman occupation that such links, first made during the relatively transient presence of military units, were strengthened into a long-term relationship, an officer of the army organising local industrial enterprise to suit military needs, and army contracts boosting demand. This is, of course, hypothesis, but will be considered in more detail later.

The evidence that we have relating to the actual formation of the town is slight, but suggests that it was established and grew rapidly at the onset of the second century (*c.*AD 100–150), at the end of the period of indirect military control that we are postulating *(16)*. There has been no modern excavation in the walled area at the heart of the town, but excavation in the suburbs to the north and south of the heart of the town gives us clues, and these, combined with an analysis of the plan of the town, have allowed the identification of four key stages of growth. It is clear from looking at the plan that the town is not arranged on a grid pattern like many other Roman towns, but is a 'ribbon' settlement. The 'main street' that ran approximately north–south through Durobrivae was Ermine Street, and the

15 The Nene, close to the point at which Ermine Street crossed the river

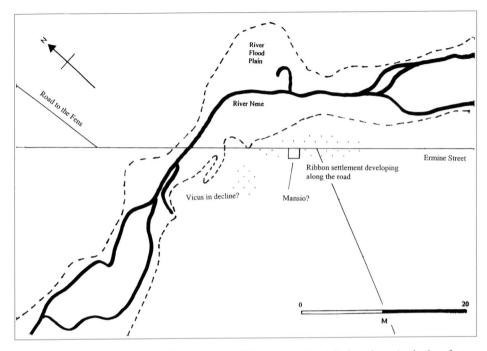

River
Flood
Plain

Road to the Fens

River Nene

Ermine Street

Ribbon settlement developing
along the road

Vicus in decline?

Mansio?

0   20

M

16 Generalised map of the early development of the town, as it might have been in the late first
or early second century

town clearly started life as a small settlement with 'frontage properties' either side
of a road. These would have been properties built on strips of land, a narrow front
on the road, perhaps to provide a shop front, but with the buildings long and thin,
stretching back from the road itself. This type of development had been identified
occurring in the suburbs (sites called Kate's Cabin and Normangate Field) during
the second and third centuries. This being the case, it is not unreasonable to
suppose that such development began in the heart of the occupied area some time
earlier, perhaps in the early second or very late first century. We will look at this
phase in detail later, but for now we should note that this is the period when the
town began to develop rapidly.

As already noted, the lack of excavation in the town makes it almost as hard
to understand Durobrivae's development in the second century as in any other
period. However, we do know that what was a minor settlement, springing up
close to a fort and the major road of Ermine Street in the late first century, grew
to become a thriving town over the next hundred years or so *(17)*. For this period
of growth we at least possess some idea of the layout of the town, information
that comes mostly from crop marks revealed through aerial photography and
compiled by the Nene Valley Research Committee from over a thousand individual images. Of course information gathered in this way and placed on the
town plan dates from all of the periods in which Durobrivae was inhabited *(11)*.
The challenge is to unravel which features on the plan belong to which period.

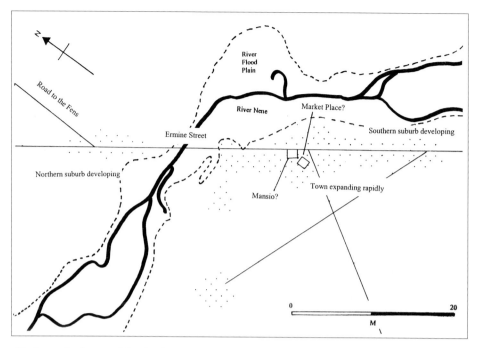

17 Generalised map of the developments in the town in the second century

This is a difficult task, but it is possible to sketch out a history of the town in the second century with the aid of the very limited amounts of excavation on the fringes of the settlement.

Second-century Durobrivae consisted of three main areas: the heart of the town (essentially the area later to be enclosed by the defences) and two principal suburbs. One of these suburbs straggled along Ermine Street to the south of the town centre, parts of which were excavated by M.V. Taylor in the 1950s. The other grew up in the Normangate Field, north of the town, and on the far side of the River Nene, and was investigated by Dannell and Wild in the 1960s and 1970s. These suburbs are important to our understanding of Durobrivae: although most of the major buildings that we know of are in what became the walled area, this measures only about 20ha (44 acres), whereas the area of the whole town is as much as 120ha (300 acres). We will begin by looking at the heart of Durobrivae, but the suburbs will provide important supporting information to allow us to paint a picture of the town as a whole.

Within the broad period of the second century, we can see at least three phases of building and development in the core area of the town. As mentioned earlier, the early town was built along Ermine Street, with rectangular plots of land running back from narrow fronts on the thoroughfare itself. Two large buildings are visible in the plan of the town, one bigger than the other. The smaller of the two has one side running along the road, and is thought to belong to this early period of development, and is commonly identified as a *mansio* (an official guest house providing accommodation for those engaged upon official business). If so, it is easy to see how the little town had grown up, perhaps the people living here prospering from their location at a river crossing on a navigable watercourse, but also on a major road running from London to York, with official traffic passing through.

The second phase of Durobrivae's expansion is marked by the development of the tangle of small, twisting roads and lanes behind the principal façade along Ermine Street. These grew as, presumably, the town became a success, attracting more local people to live there. This success is further marked by the appearance of the second, and larger, major building which can be seen in the crop marks. It is in the vicinity of the first, but set back from the Ermine Street front and at angles to it. This suggests that it was constructed behind the street front, but probably after the buildings along the street had already been constructed – and so belonging to this later period. This is possibly a *forum*, the market place and administrative centre of a Roman town, which would be a highly unusual structure in a settlement of this size, but given its plan there are few other convincing possibilities. We can envisage a town then, perhaps by the mid-second century, spreading either side of Ermine Street, acting as a market place for much of the territory around it, goods, animals and people arriving by river and by road, market time periodically swelling the already growing population.

Numerous other, smaller, buildings sprang up along the network of side streets. Many of these structures, particularly early on, must have been small and relatively poor, except in the south-east of what was later to become the walled area. Here, located at the ends of lanes running down towards the river from Ermine Street *(19)*, were some buildings of a different kind. These appear to be large, wealthy town houses, and might be those identified by the antiquary Artis in the early nineteenth century. These residences would have been finely appointed, with marbled walls, and might have been the town residences of the local elite (some boasting river views!), perhaps belonging to landowners with estates in the surrounding countryside.

The last phase of activity, which might be dated to the second (or early third) century, is the construction of the walls themselves *(20)*. It is clear from the way that some roads appear to be interrupted by the walls that the defences were laid out across a pre-existing road layout. These defences seem to have been built ruthlessly around the core of the town, truncating roads, and possibly demolishing buildings. As a result the road system seems to have been re-modelled to create an 'inner ring-road' running around the inside of the walls and connecting all the side streets that ran out off Ermine Street. A traveller up Ermine Street would now have approached through straggling suburbs, towards the defences, passing through a gateway, before reaching the bustling heart of the town, with its market place and *mansio*, elegant town houses and crooked back streets *(21)*.

But what of the suburbs? The southern suburb was the subject of small-scale excavation by Taylor in the 1950s, who concentrated upon an area between 83m

18 A building in the modern village of Water Newton, close to the site of the town. Note the use of local stone for walling and roofing – Roman buildings in the area were often constructed using similar materials, and so may have had a similar appearance

19 Approximate site of the high-status domestic buildings in the southern part of the town

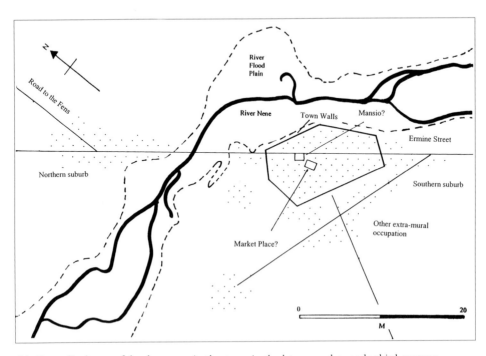

20 Generalised map of developments in the town in the late second or early third century

21 Distant view of the south of Durobrivae, as a traveller coming north up Ermine Street may have experienced it in the early third century. Note the distant plume of smoke from the industries operating in the northern suburb. Illustration by Melanie Cameron

and 457m from the town's defences. This area seems to have been first occupied at the end of the first century, with timber buildings being constructed facing onto Ermine Street. Eleven buildings were excavated by Taylor, five being interpreted as 'strip buildings', rectangular structures with a narrow front on the road. These buildings were rebuilt in stone in the later second, perhaps early third century, at about the same time the town walls were constructed *(22)*. The crop marks, however, demonstrate that these structures were only a small part of a much wider complex of roads and buildings which grew up around the edges of the town. The road running south-west to Irchester is quite clearly lined with long rectangular enclosures, which may also be the sites of such buildings, and there are many other enclosures of various sizes laid out on this side of the town, some of which might be animal pens, perhaps used for corralling animals being brought to market. Between the town and the river were two other areas of occupation, one being the site of the first-century fort (where a series of enclosures seems to extend someway to the west). The second is the stretch of Ermine Street running from the point at which it leaves the defences, to the Nene bridge, where buildings seem to front the street, as they did in the town proper. The history of these areas of occupation remains a mystery, but given the rise of the town over the second century it seems likely that they grew as the core of the settlement did, spreading along the surrounding roads as Durobrivae became a more developed urban centre.

22 Close view of the southern gate through Durobrivae's defences, from Ermine Street, as it passes through the southern suburb. *Illustration by Melanie Cameron*

On the far side of the Nene was another suburb, located in the Normangate Field area. This was arranged around a triangle of roads, and was furnished with its own maze of irregular streets. Like other areas of the city, this suburb shows traces of development through the second century, but here we also have the presence of industry – particularly the production of pottery and the smelting of iron. The pottery kilns seem to have been spread right across the northern suburb, beginning in the second century with simple bonfire kilns, but later becoming more sophisticated. Several furnaces have also been found here, offering evidence of iron working in this industrial area of the town. A traveller down Ermine Street or up the Nene would, in all likelihood, have seen clouds of smoke produced by these industries, hanging over this northern extension of Durobrivae – perhaps explaining why this area grew up on the far side of the river to the main settlement, keeping the pollution of this activity at arm's length from the core of the town.

However, kilns and furnaces are not the only thing to have been found in Normangate, and there always seems to have been occupation here as well. Small-scale excavation has explored two circular and three rectangular buildings, one of which eventually acquired wall paintings and a tessellated floor. Another of the rectangular buildings was built with a front on Ermine Street, constructed at some point in the second century over the top of some of the earlier bonfire pottery kilns. It was no mean structure, with stone footings and measuring 25m by 13m. North of this (some 250m away), an area of enclosures has been examined archaeologically, again giving evidence of second-century expansion, with the laying of a metalled track, and the spread of enclosures (first ditched, then fenced) that may have been animal pens.

It is difficult to tie developments in different areas of the settlement into a wider picture of Durobrivae, but what we can say is that the town changed beyond all recognition in the second century. In the heart of Durobrivae public building works provided a *mansio* and a *forum*, side streets expanded, and high-quality housing was built in some parts of the town. To the south, strip buildings spread down Ermine Street, and to the west buildings developed along the road to Irchester, and enclosures and buildings clustered around the site of the old fort. Buildings also lined the road towards the River Nene and the bridge across it, and on the far side, in the Normangate Field area, industry mingled with occupation. Finally, at the end of the century, or possibly at the beginning of the next, the town walls were constructed, marking out the core of the settlement. Durobrivae had grown from little more than a village to a fully-fledged town in only a hundred years.

But what of the later history of the town? Again, much of our information comes from the suburbs, especially to the north. In Normangate Field, sites away from Ermine Street seem to have remained agricultural, but open settlement appears to be in decline, even perhaps by the late second, or early third, century *(23)*. By contrast, areas closer to the road 'infilled', plots amongst workshop buildings being occupied by kilns and furnaces – a situation which lasted until the end of the Roman occupation in the early years of the fifth century. However, slightly to the east of this, commercial and industrial activity was superseded by an elaborate aisled building, and in the fourth century a mausoleum. Three circular

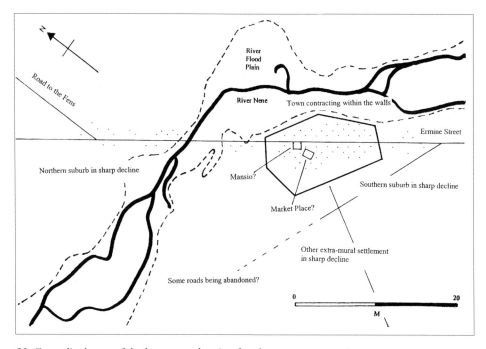

23 Generalised map of the late town, showing fourth-century contraction

33

buildings, dating to the third century, were also discovered, and identified as possible shrines (as was the contemporary phase of a nearby rectangular structure). This identification, however, is best treated with caution, given the lack of direct evidence to support it. There was, perhaps, a decline in the industrial activity in this part of the town in the late Roman period, as other sites further from the town (although still relatively close) developed, but this may be because the area had developed as a more residential area. The occupation of the northern suburb during the later history of the town was complex and mixed, but clearly supports the suggestion that the town in general was economically thriving.

A vibrant town economy is also indicated by the extent of local industry in the area in the later Roman period, with pottery production evident upstream of the town at Sibson and Stibbington, and downstream towards the edge of the Fens, at Stanground *(24)*. Iron working was also a key activity, with smelting sites being identified to the west and north-west of Durobrivae, particularly concentrated at Bedford Purlieus. Some commentators have noted that it is hard to establish where the urban settlement ends, and the industry/countryside begins, but that under-lines the curious nature of the late town – economically well developed, a sprawling settlement with many loose industrial areas around it. Also within the immediate vicinity of the town, almost part of the town itself, perhaps, were two large structures to the west, a courtyard villa located at Mill Hill, and the vast complex uncovered by Artis at Castor, considered to be a large villa, or possibly even the residence of important officials.

The final aspect of urban development in this period is, of course, the two large square buildings located in the walled area. The function of these buildings is important to our understanding of the working of the town in this later period. The smallest of the two, which has been interpreted as a *mansio*, a government stopping station or 'roadside inn', associated with the imperial post, would be available for those travelling on official business, and might have housed horses to be put at the disposal of those carrying important messages. The building is also associated with a precinct which may be the location of the town's temple. The presence of this building was mentioned in relation to the early phases of the town's development, perhaps being a contributing factor to the growth of the town, but by the late Roman period (the late third and fourth centuries), the large *mansio*, surrounded by a major settlement, must have become a significant stopping place on the roads north, and this will have continued to raise the profile of Durobrivae. The second, larger structure, also already touched upon, is that which has been interpreted as a market building or small *forum*. Either way, this structure and the courtyard which it enclosed was, by the late Roman period, clearly the market focus for all of the produce orignating from the surrounding landscape, be that pottery and worked iron from the west, or salt, salt meat, fish, fowl or basketry coming in from the Fens.

We have very little evidence about the final phases of the town's life, and as for earlier periods the lack of excavation from within the walls means that our chief

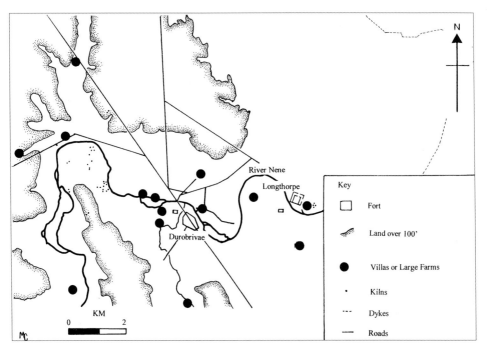

24 Durobrivae in its local landscape, showing roads and villas. *After Wild, 1974. Illustration by* Melanie Cameron

source of information is, once again, the excavations of the suburbs, and that to the north, Normangate Field, in particular. In Normangate Field there is evidence of contraction, with some of the more northerly plots falling vacant some time in the early 300s, suggesting that decline of the town began rapidly after the passing of its third-century heyday. Coins of Valentinian and the continued maintenance of drainage ditches attest to late occupation, but the mausoleum, mentioned earlier, is significant, suggesting that this area was being turned over to the burial of the dead, rather than industry and full occupation. To the south it appears that by the mid-fourth century (AD 350), there were also signs of contraction and disuse, with many structures abandoned by this time. There is also evidence of burial here, with inhumations taking place close to the defences – reinforcing the impression of decline in the suburb in the later years of the fourth century, it was perhaps all but completely abandoned by the early fifth. Occupation did continue in some form, however, though perhaps at a much reduced scale, indicated by late coins recovered during excavation. If the suburbs experience sharp decline, what was happening in the now walled urban core? We know that the central part of the town, the part contained within the defences, must still have been functioning as a viable urban centre, even after the loss of the suburbs. We know this both from direct evidence (finds from within the defended area), and more indirect indications. The most significant late find from the defended area is the Water Newton treasure, a large collection of objects associated with Christianity and probably dating from the fourth century (see cover illustration). Their exact significance we will consider in a moment, but for now it is enough to say that they indicate continued activity within the town at this date, and that given the wealth of the hoard, people of status were still living there or at least still frequenting the area. There is also the Water Newton hoard, a collection of around thirty coins which date from AD 300–350, which, like the treasure, suggests that wealth was still present in the town in the late fourth century.

These indications of wealth are not the only hints of continued town life that we have; there is also indirect evidence of the fourth-century mosaic school. There is no evidence for this school directly in the town, but distribution of mosaics in a particular style in the surrounding villas and towns (clustered mostly in the triangle formed by Lincoln, Leicester and Durobrivae) strongly suggest that a thriving industry and design school for these luxury floors was focused upon Durobrivae. The height of this industry seems to have come at some point between AD 350 and 380, indicating that the town must have retained some regional economic significance into the latter stages of the fourth century.

The town may also have come to acquire the function of a tax collection centre. During the early Roman period in Britain, the province was divided by the Romans into various regions based upon the Iron Age tribal territories. Such a unit of administration in the province was referred to as a *civitas*, and each *civitas* had a capital, located in the most significant pre-Roman tribal centres. Tax collection under the early empire would have been centralised upon these *civitas* capitals; in the case of Durobrivae, this would have been Leicester. However, an empire-wide crisis of the third century, both military and economic, seriously undermined the value of Roman currency, and the authorities resorted to collecting much tax in kind (the *annonae*) (25). This tax tended to be collected at a variety of local centres – the collection of tax thus shifting away from the *civitas* capitals. Durobrivae would probably have been one such local centre, taking part in the collection of the *annonae* by the second half of the third century (26). This administrative activity, ensuring that the inhabitants of both the urban settlement and its rural hinterland met their tax obligations to the provincial authorities, would have been highly important to the town. It would have attracted people in to pay the tax that they owed, and this would have ensured a degree of activity which may have continued to support the market element of Durobrivae's economy. This is an issue also connected to the wealthy owners of the many villas that existed close to the town, and will be considered in more detail later. However, at present it should be said that these villa owners were the group of people most probably responsible for running the town, and for financing much of the building at its heart. In this later period, when, as we shall see, the interest of wealthy landowners in 'town' life, and in spending their own personal wealth upon the town, seems generally to have been declining across many parts of the empire, the administrative function of collecting tax was important to the town's continued prosperity.

25 Shetland sheep of the type farmed during the Roman period. When tax was collected in kind it would have taken the form of livestock and other goods, presenting considerable practical problems in terms of collection. These Shetlands live at Flag Fen, Peterborough

We know little about the final abandonment of Durobrivae, but we can infer the general course of events from indirect evidence. Turning once more to excavation in the suburbs, we know that these outlying areas had contracted and were in the process of being abandoned in the fourth century. By the very end of the Roman occupation, in the first decade of the fifth century (400–410), these suburbs may well have virtually vanished, with occupation now concentrated within the defended area. When the province collapsed, the town was abandoned. With no provincial authorities for which to collect tax, the town's administrative functions would probably have ended relatively suddenly. We also know that the industries focused upon the town also ended rapidly in the post-Roman era – the Nene Valley potteries, for example, vanished almost immediately. Without the town performing its function as a provincial administrative centre, its role as a market centre would have also declined. Any connection with the army and army supply, always a main supporting factor in the scale of industry around Durobrivae, would have also come to a sharp end as the army withdrew. Industries, then, which were heavily reliant upon fulfilling military requirements, would have lost their principal consumer overnight. Life continued in much of the surrounding countryside, illustrated by evidence of Anglo-Saxon occupation from sites like Orton Hall Farm. It is even possible that the farm itself continued as a 'going

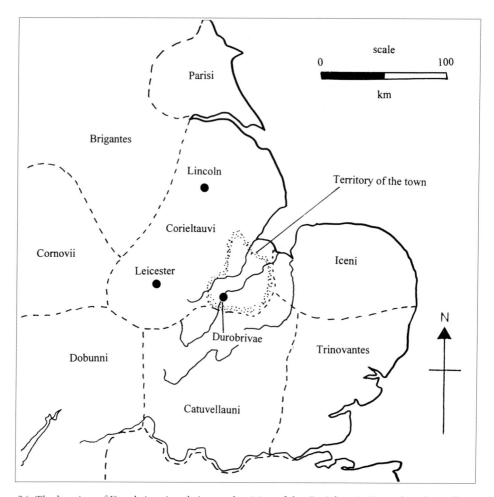

26 The location of Durobrivae in relation to the *civitas* of the Corieltauvi. *Civitas boundaries after Jones and Mattingly, 1990, with adjustments*

concern', but the Fens were swiftly abandoned, and without the wider economic structure of industries and markets, Durobrivae itself was never reoccupied.

The site of the town is, even today, a green field, underlining the fact that once the industries had gone, the settlement lost its significance *(28)*. Towns like London survived, or at least the sites that the Romans had chosen for their occupation found later significance, and the settlements were reborn. But Durobrivae died with the Roman departure, and it is hard to say exactly why. Perhaps the strong connection with the army gave the life of the town and the scale of its economy a certain artificiality – it was a town that grew because of a particular stimulus, the Roman army, a stimulus with relevance to one time in history which was never to be repeated. Durobrivae was a 'Roman town' in the full sense of the word, not a settlement, like many others, with a history and a life that transcended Roman Britain.

There are a few other aspects of our evidence for Durobrivae that cannot easily be set into this chronological framework, due to our lack of specific dating evidence for both general phases of development across the town, and the history of particular structures, but which still need to be considered. These aspects are the religious life of Durobrivae, and its places of burial. If, as noted above, the courtyard next to the *mansio* has been correctly identified as a temple precinct, we know that the town was home to a relatively large religious site. This is not unusual for Roman towns, and indeed we might expect to find such a site in a town the size of Durobrivae. We do not know how the temple developed, or which gods were worshipped there, and finds of statues of Hercules, Ceres and Minerva, as well as an inscription possibly dedicated to Mars, need not be directly associated with a temple complex. There is also the suggestion that three circular buildings identified in the northern Normangate Field suburb of the town may have had a religious function, but the lack of any finds of a religious nature from these structures makes this identification very speculative.

In the latter part of the Roman occupation, we have evidence of Christian religion from the town: the famous Water Newton treasure (see cover illustration). The treasure consists of twenty-eight objects, many of which bear the Christian Chi-Rho symbol. The exact find spot of the treasure is unknown, and so we can

27 Roman pottery from the Nene Valley industry. *Reproduced courtesy of Peterborough Museum and Art Gallery*

28 Looking west from the edge of the walled area of the town. This field would have been covered with a spread of settlement by the third century AD

say little about the treasure in terms of, for example, the specific part of the town in which it was located. The general significance of the treasure is that it demonstrates a Christian presence in Durobrivae in the fourth century, but without knowing where the treasure came from, it is hard to say what kind of presence the treasure indicates. Is it, as some believe, the 'church plate' of an early church in the town? This is possible, but we have to be cautious of this interpretation as no formal church building of the Roman period has ever been conclusively demonstrated to have existed in Britain. The presence of the Christian religion in late Roman Britain seems to have taken the form of the private observance of wealthy individuals, and so it might be more likely that the treasure was the property of one person, or a wealthy family. This clearly suggests a small, but wealthy Christian community in the town, though not one that was necessarily central to the life of Durobrivae.

A final, but important, element of the Roman town that we have so far only touched upon is its places of burial. It was practice to bury the dead, or to intern the urns containing the ashes of the dead after cremation, along the main roads approaching the town. What was probably the main cemetery of the town was located to the south-west, between Ermine Street and the road that branches off it to skirt west of the defended area of the town. The antiquarians Stukeley and Artis noted urn burials and stone coffins south of the road that ran out of the town's north-west gate (close to Ermine Street as it ran towards the crossing point of the Nene), and Artis also discovered burials on the south-east corner of the defended area, facing the River Nene. There are also areas of burial associated with the northern suburb at Kate's Cabin and Normangate Field, infant burials discovered associated with the southern suburb, and possible (but unconfirmed) mausoleum structures along the road to Irchester. We can say little about the chronology of these cemeteries, beyond the rather general observation that cremation was a predominantly early practice (second- and perhaps early third-century activity) and burials (the many stone coffins found around the town, for example) indicate later (third-, fourth- and fifth-century) activity. This being the case, it seems likely that the main burial ground, lying south-west of the town, was in fairly consistent use throughout the period when the town was occupied, but the burial ground facing the river, on the south-east corner of the defended area, was perhaps mainly used in the later Roman period. Cemeteries associated with the northern suburbs may have fallen out of use as those suburbs contracted in the late Roman period.

This, then, is the sum total of our direct evidence about the town of Durobrivae. But as we have already seen, when considering the town's role as a focal point for more widespread interests, like the pottery industry, salt production, iron working and the mosaic school, indirect evidence can throw light upon the developing economic interests of the town, even when direct evidence is lacking. In the chapters that follow we shall try to understand what was occurring in the hinterland of Durobrivae and, in doing so, we will not only locate the town in the wider landscape (physical, social and economic) in which it existed, but we will also learn more about the town itself.

29 The site of the town today – Durobrivae is a scheduled monument ensuring that the ground cannot be disturbed by ploughing, or even archaeological investigation, in case the archaeology of the town is damaged. The site remains largely under pasture

However, there is also another way of exploring the evidence that we have – what would it have seemed like to one of the people who was actually there, one of the inhabitants of Roman Britain? In asking ourselves this question, we can help to pull together fragments of information that can often seem disconnected, and begin to see that evidence as pieces of a whole. A traveller up Ermine Street in the late second century, for example, would have approached through sprawling suburbs, towards the defences. With the industrial areas of the northern suburb developing, perhaps even from the south side of the town, smoke would be seen rising from pottery kilns and iron-processing furnaces. We know that anyone approaching the town now would have had to pass through a gateway in the new walls, up the main road lined with narrow-fronted shops (buildings maybe two storeys high), before reaching the bustling heart of the town, with its market place and *mansio*, elegant town houses and winding backstreets. In its heyday, Durobrivae would have seen many visitors, people passing through on business, or traders bringing goods to market from the wider territory of the town. As we explore that wider territory, we will return to one such traveller, a pot peddler – the kind of 'independent trader' that may have walked the roads of Roman Britain trying to make a living. By following one man on his journey through the hinterland, we will get a better idea of what that landscape was like.

3

THE CENTRAL FEN TERRITORIES

The rise and fall of the town is only one part of the story of Durobrivae. At its height in the second and third centuries, roads radiated out from it in all directions, and up those roads came the produce and people that kept the town fed and functioning. Pottery, salt, agricultural produce, iron ore and finished goods all made their way into the market place. But what lay up those roads as they ran out into the territory of the town? Where did the people and things come from that thronged Durobrivae on market day? To the east lie the Fens *(7* and *8)*. The Fens have traditionally been understood as a whole, a single landscape stretching from modern Peterborough in the west to Kings Lynn in the east, Cambridge in the south, and the Wash in the north. This understanding of the Fens has underpinned the way in which generations of scholars (from Dugdale, writing in 1772, and Stukeley, 1776, all the way to the modern day) have interpreted what happened in the area under Roman rule, but is something which we need to re-examine before considering its relationship with Durobrivae. It has particular relevance to any consideration of the Fens as an imperial estate, as this raises important questions about the nature of Roman land ownership. We know from other parts of the empire that an active land market existed, so land will have changed hands, and large blocks like the putative Fenland estate would, over time, be broken up through the natural working of that market. Fragments of land will have been bought or sold, land confiscated from imperial enemies and land grants made to imperial friends. We know from the evidence available from other regions of the empire that Roman estates were often not large open tracts, but many small individual properties, or different properties in widely separated locations that collectively formed the 'estate' of a wealthy landowner or even the emperor. A Roman senator in the second century AD might, for example, own villas on the coast of Italy, as well as working farms, have land holdings in Africa, perhaps Spain, and maybe even Britain. The fragmented nature of such estates, perhaps better considered as the 'property portfolios' of the rich, would, of course, have made it even

30 The Fen Edge. Note the sudden rise of the ground in the background, illustrating the abrupt end of the Fenland. This very obvious change in the landscape at the Fen Edge has led many to consider the Fens as a whole – but this ignores the complexity of developments within the Fenland

easier for individual elements of such 'portfolios' to change hands. Thus the idea that large monolithic blocks of land might remain permanently in either private or imperial ownership is unrealistic.

Another key element, upon which the identification of the Fens as an imperial estate rests, is that of imperial monopolies. Salt production is commonly seen as such a monopoly, which means that that it was directly controlled by the central authority of the empire – the imperial household. It must be noted that this is not universally accepted: salt making was a common practice, and is seen by some as being too widespread to have been effectively controlled in this way. However, this idea has been used to reinforce the notion that the Fens were an imperial estate – they were a major focus for salt production, and therefore, the argument goes, the area must have been owned by the imperial authorities. However, this suggestion ignores the fact that direct ownership is not the only model that we know of for the running of such monopolies. An important concept in the ancient world for the administration of many such aspects of imperial business is 'contracting'. We see this situation in taxation. The central government knew how much tax it required from a particular province, but rather than setting up a complex bureau-cracy to collect it, it simply contracted a group of individuals to collect the tax upon the government's behalf. Any extra that these 'tax farmers', as the contractors were called, could collect, they could keep. However bad from the point of view of the citizen (such a situation inevitably led to extortion over and above the official level of tax, as this represented the tax collector's profit), this was a very efficient arrangement as far as the central government was concerned. Tax was delivered up front, and in its entirety, without the need to maintain an expensive tax-collecting machine. Thus, even were salt production to be accepted as being indicative of an imperial monopoly, if something as central to the functioning of the state as tax could have been 'farmed out', it is more than probable that local salt production would be contracted out in a similar way. Thus the central government would avoid responsibility for directly running the salt works, whilst still gaining profit from the production of salt.

One last argument is often raised to reinforce the idea that the Fens were an imperial estate: the lack of villas in the area. Across the expanse of the Fens there are very few structures that could be considered 'wealthy' buildings, a situation which might imply that there was no local 'middle class', no local landlords, or wealthy farmers. What such a situation might suggest is that the landscape was inhabited by a large mass of socially undifferentiated farmers, and that the only authority that was powerful enough to act as 'landlord' to such a large area would be the emperor. The inhabitants of the Fens would be 'share croppers', working the land and handing over a proportion of their crop to the imperial authorities as rent. As we will see in the Central Fens, however, there are more ways of demonstrating wealth and prestige than architecture of a 'Roman' style. Moreover, we shall see in the next chapter, when we examine the evidence from the Silt Fens, there are signs of different levels of wealth and prestige in the area, even if the distinctions are subtle. We should also bear in mind that, if an area is generally poor, those in that area need only demonstrate that they are relatively well off to be considered wealthy in that region. What we need to look for in the Fens, and other such areas, is not villas (often interpreted to indicate wealth and status at the top of the social hierarchy), but settlements that are simply wealthier than those around them. In the context of the Fens, where most sites are relatively poor and show little sign of architecture more substantial than thatched roofs and wattle-and-daub walls, a building with straight walls and a tiled roof carries greater significance than it would if it were, for example, located in a landscape of more elaborate stone-built structures. When viewed in this way, we shall see that there are indeed some relatively wealthy sites on the Fens, even if they do not look like villas.

On several counts, then, we can see that the idea of a single, monolithic imperial estate in the Fens is flawed. The action of the land market would have broken up any such entity relatively quickly, and both local salt production and lack of villas can be seen to be less supportive of the idea than has previously been considered to be the case. There may, as we shall see later, have been a greater degree of interest in the Fenland region by the Roman authorities than was perhaps normal, but this does not prove that most of the landscape was under their

31 This modern road (the A605), follows the approximate route of the Fen Causeway at this point, near the village of Coates

direct control – and, if we consider the Fens in this way, we must also consider how it was linked with the town of Durobrivae.

If we follow the road which runs east from Durobrivae, we are following a road that we call the Fen Causeway, a road that runs through the Iron Age and Roman site of Fengate, a large Fen Edge settlement, and then out into what, in Roman times, would have been the peaty wastelands of southern Fenland *(31)*. The road ultimately ends up in Norfolk; running deep into the territory of the Iceni, but much of the ground that it crossed in Roman times was empty, too wet to be habitable. However, in the midst of this wetness was a group of 'islands', areas of gravel just a little higher than the surrounding landscape, but high enough to be dry, and these island outposts of the uplands attracted settlement. Indeed, they were inhabited well before the Roman Conquest, and well before the Silt Fens to the north. They were, as we shall see, distinct from the rest of Fenland in many ways, and deserve to be considered separately.

The awareness of pre-Roman activity in this area has been steadily growing over recent decades. Problems have dogged our understanding of late Iron Age settlement here (and elsewhere in the Fens), and it is as well to be aware of these before considering what we do know. A major problem is dating. Pottery is the tool most commonly used by archaeologists to establish a chronology for sites, as it survives in the ground, and can usually be dated fairly closely. Pottery evidence from the Fens has suggested that, whilst there was early and mid-Iron Age activity, there was virtually no occupation during the late Iron Age which is the period of interest to us as it is 'late Iron Age' Britain that the Romans invaded. However, it has recently become apparent that the Central Fens were conservative in their pottery use. In effect, they continued to use mid-Iron Age pottery into the late Iron Age period. This means that many sites considered to be mid-Iron Age, dated largely on the kind of pottery that they were using, might in fact have been occupied in the late Iron Age as well, and have been occupied when the Romans made their way into the region in about AD 47. A second problem is the siting of modern towns. Iron Age settlement concentrated on the 'Fen islands', the slightly higher ground, helping the settlements to avoid flooding. Modern settlements have been sited in the same positions for similar reasons, and consequently modern Fenland towns like March, and other modern features of the landscape like prisons and marshalling yards, obscure the early history of the region

That said, the activities of the *Fen Survey* have collected considerable information in this area, and we are now in a position to piece together a picture of life in the Central Fens on the eve of the Roman Conquest. The most prominent sign of pre-Roman occupation in this area is that of Stonea Camp *(32)*. The Camp is a large D-shaped earthwork on Stonea Island. There were multiple phases of activity on this site, the earthworks being remodelled several times, but the final occupation seems to date to the very late Iron Age and early Roman period, perhaps lasting until no later than around AD 60. The Iron Age coinage of this period found in the Central Fen area is predominantly Icenian – this area seems to have been dominated by that tribe, but the camp is only the last in a sequence of monuments in this area. Activity here stretches back to the Neolithic, suggesting that the area had a strong ritual identity, perhaps developing over millennia. This isn't surprising, as water and wet places have carried religious connotations in many periods *(33)*, and this very watery location may have been imbued with a high degree of significance for the inhabitants. The camp, although often interpreted as a 'fort', is not really sited or designed to perform this role. The ramparts face inland, with the side facing the water open. As anyone entering the area to attack this structure would, given that it is on the edge of an island, have to come by boat, its defences are non-existent in precisely the one direction from which such an attack could come. We must thus reconsider its identification as a defensive structure. An alternative interpretation of the site is as a ritual enclosure – a large monument built by the community that lived in the Central Fens, a place to meet as a community, and to perform the rituals that bound them together. This interpretation has the merit of placing the Stonea Camp site in the context of all the other religious monuments from previous periods that were built on Stonea Island, and also making sense of the architecture of the monument. Impressive ramparts would have faced into the island, from where members of the community would come, with the open side facing out to the spiritually important water of the Fens. It is also possible that the effort needed to construct Stonea Camp was considered worthwhile because, over and above the ritual

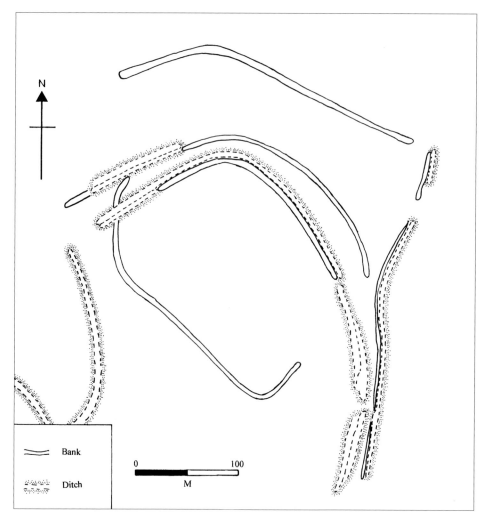

32 Plan of the late Iron Age site of Stonea Camp, an earthwork located on a gravel island in the Central Fens. *After Jackson and Potter, 1997. Illustration by Melanie Cameron*

significance of the site, the presence of a major structure here sent a powerful message of domination to any one who might challenge Icenian power in the area.

Such a monument clearly had great importance for the settlements around it *(34)*. Evidence for ordinary 'domestic' sites is slim, but sites where occupation has been confirmed in this period are confined to the higher and more stable gravel islands within this area. We can say little about these sites – only small amounts of pottery have been recovered, and there is no detailed excavation of a late Iron Age settlement. However, it seems likely that, as with other areas of England at this time, ordinary occupation was in the form of individual households. We might envisage small farmsteads scattered across the landscape, run by families that met and rein-forced their sense of identity as a community at monuments like Stonea Camp.

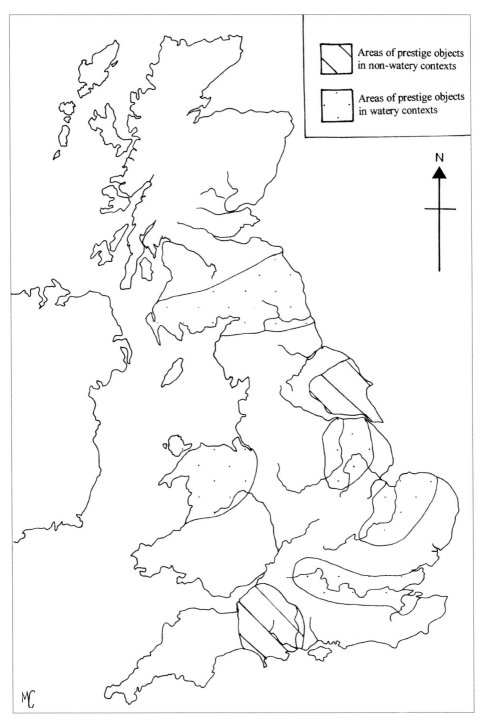

33 A map showing regional traditions of the deposition of 'prestige' objects – objects that would probably have only been owned by the wealthy, like, for example, metal bracelets – during the Iron Age. *After Wait, 1985. Illustration by Melanie Cameron*

Areas of prestige objects in non-watery contexts

Areas of prestige objects in watery contexts

N

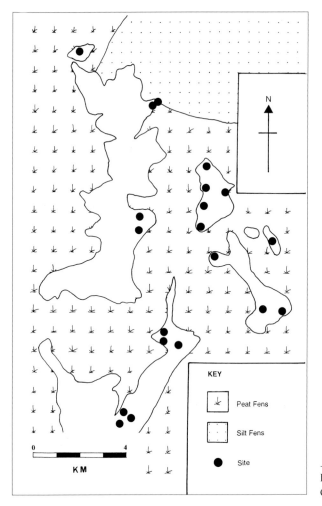

34 The distribution of probable Iron Age domestic sites in the Central Fens. *After Malim, 1992*

KEY

Peat Fens

Silt Fens

● Site

If we can place Stonea Camp at the spiritual and communal heart of this area, what of the economy of the area in the late Iron Age? Again, there is little evidence, but comparison with well-excavated sites on the Fen Edge, in particular at Fengate, now under the eastern industrial estates of Peterborough, give us an idea of how such sites were supported (*35*). With the Fens all around these islands, a key aspect of their economy must have been a range of Fenland 'produce', like fish, fowl and reeds, used for roofing and basketry. On the islands themselves, if the sites here were, as we are suggesting, broadly similar to Fengate, we might envisage a network of fields, probably used for rearing livestock, typically sheep. There may have been cultivation of crops, but this will have been limited in extent, given the low-lying, and wet nature of the ground. However, there is an important additional aspect to the Iron Age economy of the Central Fens – salt. We will consider the mechanics of producing salt later, in relation to the much larger and better-evidenced Roman period industry, but we know that salt was being exploited before the Roman occupation of the area, particularly on the Silt Fens to the north. There is limited evidence for such activity in the Central Fens, but later developments in the area under the Romans, who exploited salt in the Central Fens, suggest that salt production in the Central Fens in the late Iron Age is also a strong possibility. The apparent wealth of the area, with many silver coins being discovered at Stonea Camp, and coin hoards and objects for personal adornment deposited in watery locations around the region, perhaps as offerings to the gods, must have been generated by activity over and above agriculture. Salt production is the obvious candidate, a commodity of surprising importance in the ancient world, being one of the few ways of preserving meat before refrigeration, and providing a good-quality natural seasoning. Any area producing salt would be in a position to create wealth, either for themselves or for the people that controlled them. It may also have been the case that Stonea Camp acted as a trading 'port' and focus for the salt-production industry, bringing together traders from the territory of the Iceni to the east, but also the Corieltauvi to the west and perhaps the Catuvellauni to the south. As such it may have contributed considerably to local fortunes.

As Roman armies swept north in the middle part of the first century AD, the area seems to have been sidestepped, and in the early years of the Conquest, the king of the Iceni, Prasutagus, had secured 'client' status – he and his people were allies of Rome, and, superficially at least, remained independent. Stonea Camp was very active in this period, and large numbers of Icenian coins have been found from the site that date to the time of the client state. This independence, however, was not to last. The first sign of trouble was a minor rebellion involving only a portion of the Iceni, ending in a battle conceivably somewhere in the Fens. Stonea

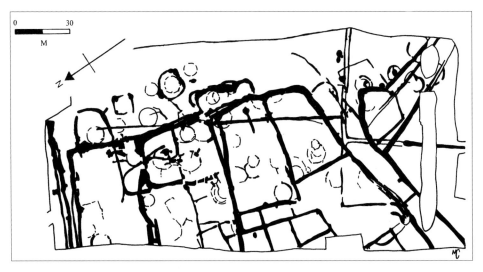

35 The site plan of Fengate, an Iron Age and Roman site on the Fen Edge. *After Pryor, 1984.*
Illustration by Melanie Cameron

Camp has even been suggested as a location for the fight. The real trouble came in AD 60, however, with the uprising we know as the Boudican Revolt.

It should be borne in mind that Durobrivae did not yet exist, but the 'Roman' geography of the area was already forming. The crossing of the Nene, where the town was later to grow, was a vital link in the communications of the Roman army as it advanced northwards, and as such it was controlled by a small fort. Also, located between the crossing and the Fen Edge, was the Fortress of Longthorpe. Its position was no mere accident, as here it guarded the Nene, looking north into the territory of the Corieltauvi, and south into the territory of the Catuvellauni. But it also looked east, into the 'independent' territory of the Iceni.

The Boudican Revolt struck the young province like a hammer blow, a blow which almost threw the Romans out of Britain. Longthorpe may well have been on the front line, a strong suggestion by the excavators being that the outline of a small fort cut into the plan of the initial, larger fortress was an emergency fortification, erected by remnants of defeated military units trying to hold out until help arrived. Here is not the place to recount a detailed history of the revolt, but simply to note that the Romans did defeat the rebels, and that in the aftermath Rome took the Icenian kingdom, and a period of harsh repression began. That repression took the form of reorganisation, both of the local communication ways, and land ownership. This is important, because it is in the post-revolt carving up of the lands of defeated tribes that the eventual territory of Durobrivae began to take shape.

As a result of the Roman annexation of eastern England, we see sudden developments in the communications of the area. The Fen Causeway was thrust out into the Central Fens and beyond *(36, 37, 38)*. It seems that the road was constructed after the revolt was over, or perhaps in the closing stages of military operations, reaching out into the Fens and allowing the movement of troops

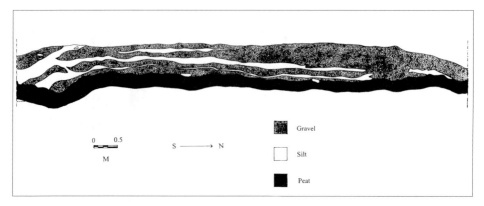

0   0.5
M

S ⟶ N

Gravel

Silt

Peat

36 A section through the Fen Causeway, dug at Flag Fen, near Peterborough. The Causeway has a complex construction, necessary for a road built across Fenland. The thick gravel base of the road is woven through with long wooden poles in a criss-cross pattern to give it both strength and flexibility, 'rafting' it over unstable peat. *Illustration by Melanie Cameron*

37 *Above* The Flag Fen section of
the Fen Causeway is exposed, and
open to the public

38 *Right* A close-up view of the
section of the Fen Causeway at Flag
Fen, showing stones laid out in the
early stages of the road's
construction to mark the route that
it would take

through an otherwise impassable landscape. It is perhaps no surprise that the road makes for the otherwise isolated and hard-to-reach settlements of the Central Fen islands – perhaps this area was considered a likely refuge for those who wished to continue the fight. In a great engineering project the road 'island hops', running across the shortest possible stretches of peat, connecting the islands that scatter the area to each other, and crucially, to the outside world.

The complex engineering of this road is worth dwelling on, as it must have required considerable effort to build, demonstrating the importance that the Romans attached to constructing a communication ways into this area. It appears that, before the revolt, fragmentary communications existed along what became the westernmost sections of the road. This must surely reflect activity based upon the Longthorpe Fortress, the army reaching into Fenland, connecting with, and perhaps informally policing, Icenian settlement on the islands. In the first decade or so after the Conquest, canals and perhaps a few small roads were constructed. These were the precursor of the Fen Causeway in the AD 60s, and it may be that the road rationalised and expanded these existing communications. Nonetheless, the construction of the Fen Causeway was a major task across the open Fens. A large linear bank of gravel was heaped up as a foundation. This bank often contained criss cross layers of thin branches to help stabilise it, and 'raft' it over unstable ground. The road, however, did more than its predecessors, not only connecting the Central Fen settlements to the western Fen Edge, but also running right out through the other side and eventually passing on into Norfolk. Once the construction was complete, the Central Fens were connected to the outside world both to the east and the west, and the Romans had a road which connected the Midlands to East Anglia, without the lengthy detour south via Cambridge that would otherwise be required *(3)*. This was clearly a major development, making the Central Fens accessible as never before – but there were also other changes taking place on the Fen islands, perhaps in part brought about by the existence of the Fen Causeway. The pottery used by the inhabitants of the islands was, until roughly the period of the Boudican revolt, of the type produced in the east, in the territory of the Iceni. After the revolt, however, it is pottery from the west that was used here. What this indicates is that once this small community, traditionally eastward looking, had been connected to the outside world, it suddenly turned to the west. Why this happened is not entirely clear, but there are some clues in the evidence.

At a place along the road called Grandford *(39)*, in about AD 61, following the Boudican Revolt, a fort was built. The fort was probably not occupied for very many years, being erected before the road (the road loops around the outside of the fort, indicating that the fort was there first). However, the presence of this fort, even for just a short time, helps us to make sense of events here. The fort suggests that after the revolt the military assumed brief responsibility for administering and policing this area – a small detachment of troops being based out in the Fens to underline the Roman occupation in a visible way. This poses the question: what

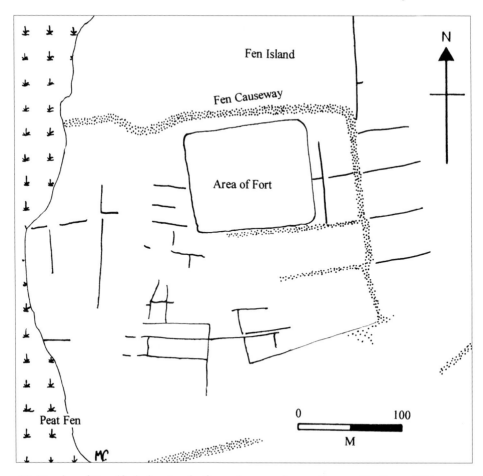

N

Fen Island

Fen Causeway

Area of Fort

Peat Fen

0   100
M

39 Site plan of Grandford, showing the fort and surrounding settlement. *After Potter, 1981.*
Illustration by Melanie Cameron

happened to the people who had traditionally ruled the area, the native elite that had led the tribe into revolt against Rome? It is probable that, in the aftermath of the revolt, the social structure of the area was severely disrupted. Those who led the revolt, the natural leaders of the tribe and of individual tribal communities, would have been prime victims of any post-revolt clampdown, either killed in battle, executed afterwards, or perhaps, in defeat, being stripped of their wealth, their property confiscated. The area must, in the first years after its annexation, have had a severely weakened native leadership, or no such leadership at all, and this provides for us a context for the period of military rule which the fort at Grandford suggests. The community in the Central Fens was too valuable to the Romans to leave it to its own devices, to slowly recover in its own time. This region produced salt, and salt was important to the advancing Roman armies, for the same reasons that it was important to the ancient world generally. The salting of meat allowed its preservation for long enough for it to be carried to wherever the army was, and the small fort at Grandford perhaps served a twofold purpose: to control a leaderless community, but also to put the local salt industry under military control. If, as we are suggesting, the salt industry was valuable to the Roman authorities, it was clearly in their interest to remove it from the 'unreliable' control of a tribe that had shown itself dangerously rebellious. Such a move also had the added benefit of punishing the Iceni by depriving them of an important source of tribal wealth. The Boudican Revolt thus appears to mark the point of a reorganisation of land owning in the area, a reorganisation which saw the Central Fens being detached from the Iceni and placed, for a transitional period, under military rule. The fort was only occupied for a short time, so the period of direct military rule was comparatively short. If, as we have suggested, after this period the Central Fens looked westwards rather than eastwards as they had previously done, it is logical to assume that once the area was released from military control and reintegrated into local tribal structures, rather than being returned to the Iceni it was in fact 're-allocated' to the Corieltauvi, the tribe to the west from which most of the pottery being used in the Central Fenland now came.

The next significant development in this area came at the start of the second century *(41)*. By this period the communications system had become well developed, and the Central Fen area had been well and truly connected to the rest of the province. Roads and canals connected the individual islands to each other, whilst a well-maintained Fen Causeway connected the area to the outside world to the east and the west. Settlements had developed across these islands, not least at Stonea where (as mentioned earlier) there was a structure that has been identified as a tower, a structure that would have dominated the region, being visible for miles around in the flat landscape. Quite what the function of this tower was, we do not know, but it has been suggested that it might have been a centre for administration in the region, playing host to a centurion with powers over government and justice, perhaps with a small detachment of soldiers and staff.

A second significant settlement lay at Grandford, which had grown up around the now abandoned fort. It is thought that Grandford began life as a *vicus* settlement, a village that grew up because there was a fort there, and probably inhabited initially by camp followers (people attracted to military establishments because of the money to be made there). The settlement, however, outlived the fort, its position directly on the Fen Causeway perhaps economically advantageous to the people there. In any case, by the mid-Roman period structures here had window glass and wall-paintings – signs of considerable wealth compared to neighbouring settlements. This is important, as we shall discover: the display of wealth in Roman Fenland was not a simple matter, and has a lot to tell us about the politics of the area.

Wealth is a significant issue. The display of wealth in the ancient world was a way of visibly asserting the place in society that it afforded you. If you were to rule, to maintain your leadership over your people, you needed to demonstrate that you

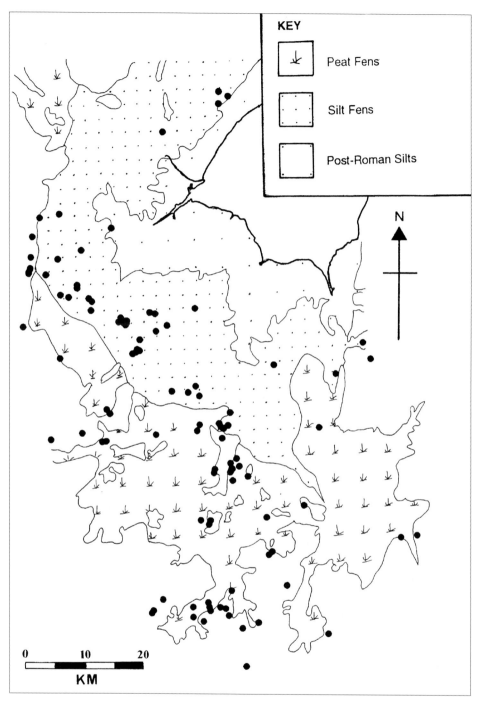

40 A map showing first-century sites. Note the cluster of sites on the islands of the Central Fens. The sites to the north, on the silts, are the nucleus of settlements from which occupation expanded in the second century

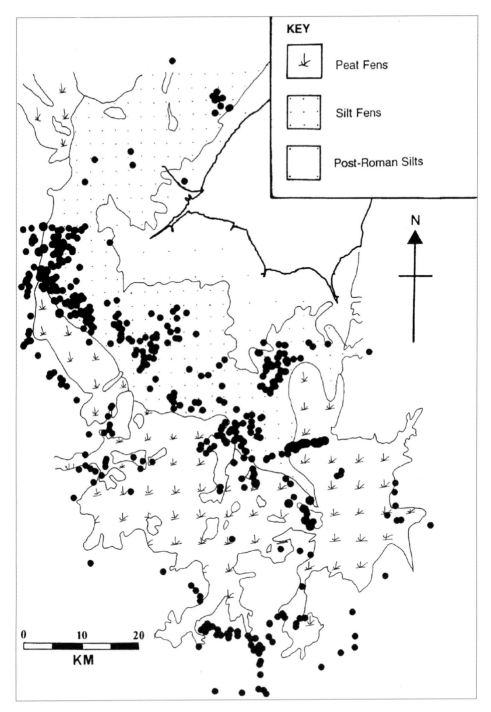

KEY

Peat Fens

Silt Fens

Post-Roman Silts

N

0   10   20
KM

41 A map showing the sites founded in the Fens during the second and third centuries

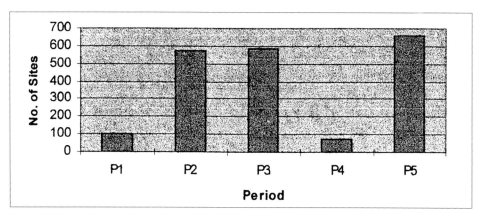

42 Graph showing the number of sites founded in the Fens (including the Fen Edge, Silts and Fen islands) in each century of the Roman occupation (Periods 1-4 being the first to the fourth century). Period 5 are sites which cannot be dated to a specific century. Note the small number of sites in the first century, and the massive expansion in the second

had the wealth needed to maintain your social role. The traditional way in which we think of this occurring in Roman Britain was through architecture – the building of 'Roman-style' buildings, for example the big villa complexes like Fishbourne or Chedworth. These villas were, like the large wealthy houses west of Durobrivae, the homes of the elite, the rulers of local society. But architecture was only one possible way of expressing status and wealth, and increasingly subtle studies of Roman period 'material culture' (the objects left behind by the people of the time, anything from pots to bracelets to houses) illustrate that architecture alone cannot give us all the answers. In the Central Fens we see not only that it was possible to display wealth in different ways, but also that it was possible for wealth to be demonstrated in several different ways in the same area at the same time *(43)*.

To begin, in an area with a strong Iron Age history, we need to go back to before the Roman Conquest. The territory of the Iceni is notable for the high occurrence of what we might term 'portable' wealth, that is precious objects. The Fens are a watery area, and a high occurrence of such objects, distributed in wet places, is a prominent Iron Age trend, with portable wealth deposited as 'votive' objects (effectively gifts to the gods). We see this tradition in general across much of the region, and in studies of Iron Age religion the Fens have been specifically singled out as an area where such deposition took place *(33)*. The use of precious objects in this way was something which could only be indulged in by the wealthy. The deposition of precious objects then becomes not just a sign of wealth (an individual *must* be wealthy to 'throw away' something valuable), but also a sign of power – if the gods require valuable gifts, only the wealthy can give them. The wealthy thus gain control over a crucial aspect of everyday life: religion. The Iron Age pattern of wealth display in the Central Fens, then, was one of portable wealth, possibly deposited for ritual ends, but certainly with a political motive involved.

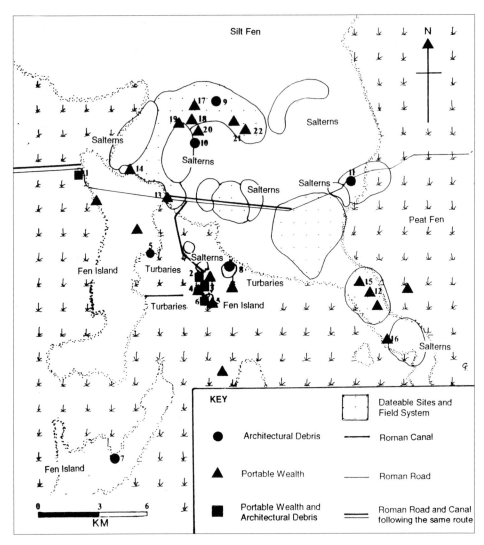

43 Generalised map of the different types of settlement and activity in the Central Fens, also showing the distribution of different types of wealth

This is significant, given that the Central Fens were the heart of Iron Age settlement in the region (44), and that the deposition of precious objects is a pattern that continues into the Roman period. Many sites in the Central Fens show evidence of portable wealth, including personal jewellery and coinage. This tradition was seemingly well engrained, as it continued in a significant way into the later Roman period. In particular, we should note that the Central Fens is one of the principal areas in Britain for the deposition of pewter hoards in the third and fourth centuries.

Much pewter, and many other items of portable wealth, have been recovered from places not directly connected to settlements – isolated finds which do not

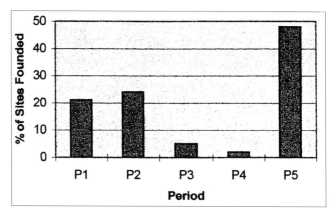

44 Graph showing the number of sites founded in the Fens islands only in each century of the Roman occupation. Note how many more sites were in existence in the first century than is generally true for the region (figure 42) – this shows the high level of occupation on the islands in the pre-Roman period

seem to have a direct relationship to the local pattern of settlement. However, we must remember that by definition the wealth belonged to a person, not a place, and unlike wealth which takes the form of elaboration to buildings (wall-paintings for example, or stone walls) portable wealth could be moved from place to place. The point, then, about portable wealth, is not to find specific sites which we can identify as 'high-status sites', but simply to note that there is a high incidence of such objects generally in a particular area, the Central Fens being one such place. The continued use of these symbols of wealth into the Roman period, even if we cannot pin them down to a specific site, infers that, quite apart from any physical continuity in the settlement pattern from the late Iron Age to the Roman period, there was also social continuity. In effect, what was considered an acceptable and legitimate way of displaying wealth before the Roman Conquest remained an acceptable way of displaying it afterwards.

Portable wealth forms only part of the story; the other part is architecture. We know little of the native tradition in the region from the Iron Age, and what we know of the buildings of such settlements in the Roman period we have learnt from a few small, and often inadequately recorded excavations, like those at Welney. The 'Welney House' is one of the best examples that we have from the area of a small, domestic structure, a range of square rooms arranged around a courtyard, with a thatched roof, and walls of 'cob', a kind of mud construction *(45)*. Although this information is scanty, it does allow us to sketch out some possible outlines for a 'native' architecture of the region. Firstly, the thatched roof is an important factor. A thatched roof does not have to sit upon a regular structure beneath. The walls can be uneven, as can be the beams that support the roof itself. The timber used to build such structures, if uneven, need not be high-quality sawn beams, but more easily acquired timber from smaller trees. In an environment like the Fens, high-quality building materials like stone, tiles, or straight timber would have been in restricted supply, and where they occurred they were almost certainly imports into the area – and thus probably expensive. Ordinary buildings such as normal domestic structures will have been constructed from more readily available

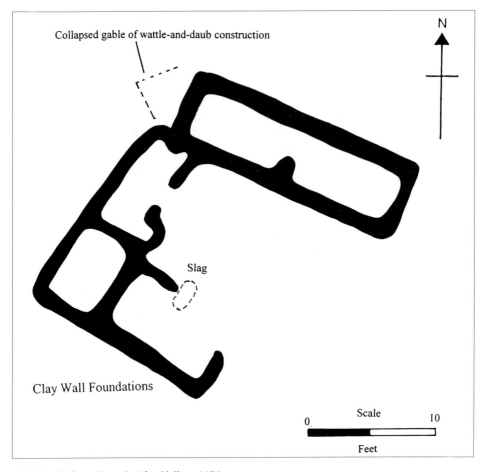

Collapsed gable of wattle-and-daub construction

N

Slag

Clay Wall Foundations

Scale

0   10

Feet

45 The 'Welney House'. *After Phillips, 1970*

local materials, and this we see at Welney. This is, of course, only a sketch. But it does allow us to make the comparison with other, very different structures that we encounter in the Fens, those where such imported building materials as tile, stone and probably straight timbers (needed to construct the regular framework required to support a tiled roof) are encountered.

Structures built of high–quality materials are essentially clustered into a handful of settlements, and we have a good idea about the nature of three of them: Grandford, Flaggrass and, of course, Stonea. The site at Grandford has no Iron Age predecessor, and, as mentioned above, it appears (judging from the coinage) to have grown up in the first century around the fort occupied during the Neronian period. This settlement became well developed by the mid-Roman period, daub -and-thatch structures being decorated internally with wall paintings and the windows being fitted with glass. The later Roman period saw the buildings of Grandford rebuilt in stone. The site here is interesting, as from the beginning there are things about it which distance it from other, more 'native' sites in the Fens.

Firstly, whilst most of the sites in the region are in marginal and isolated locations, distanced from the main stream of regional culture, Grandford grew up close to a fort, which itself was located upon a major road. Grandford thus had better communications, and more contact with the outside world, than any site ever had in this area in the Iron Age. Secondly, although some structures at the site bore a resemblance to the 'native' school of architecture when they were first constructed, they were elaborated, over time, in a style which was clearly an import from outside, bearing more resemblance to the kind of decoration that we are familiar with in villas (wall-paintings and glass windows) than in Fenland houses.

At Stonea, as we have previously considered, there is the principal structure of the tower. Constructed in the early second century, it is quite unlike any other structure in the region, native or otherwise. The amount of window glass recovered from this location is worth mentioning, as this encapsulates the extra-ordinary nature of the site – more glass was recovered from the site of the tower than from any other site in Roman Britain with the exception of Fishbourne. This is an incredible fact, considering that this was in a 'backwater' area of the province. There was also an apron of 'hard standing' laid out at the foot of the tower, which the excavators have interpreted as a market place, and one of the few possible places where a market is demonstrable in the Fenland region. A small settlement also clustered here, made up of small square buildings with a mixture of tile and thatched roofs, and, at a little distance, the settlement was provided with a temple. Thus it is not just the tower that is unusual, but also the concentration of activity around it *(46)*.

It is the case that the objects found on the site, what we might call its 'material culture', are not that rich compared to other sites of similar levels of architectural complexity in other parts of the province (like, for example, Castle Copse Villa, between Bath and Winchester). There were not, for example, as many amphorae (the large pottery vessels used to transport commodities like wine, olive oil, and fish sauce) as we might expect to find. However, we cannot consider the culture here in absolute terms – that is to say we should not be seeking a set number of amphorae before declaring the site 'Roman', or 'Official', or whatever other description we are seeking to justify. Rather, we should see it in terms relative to the area around it, the Central Fens, where we have already suggested that the penetration of 'Roman culture' was not that great. When considered like this, if we put the site of Stonea in the context of the sites around it, the material culture associated with the tower becomes extraordinarily rich. There are glass bottles, pottery, and possibly imported foodstuffs which, although present in only small quantities, are all but totally absent on other sites. How do we interpret this?

This material culture is certainly connected to the tower, as when the tower was decommissioned in the third century these objects are no longer found. Recent re-analysis of the material from this site has demonstrated that the way food was prepared here (illustrated by combining an analysis of the type of pottery

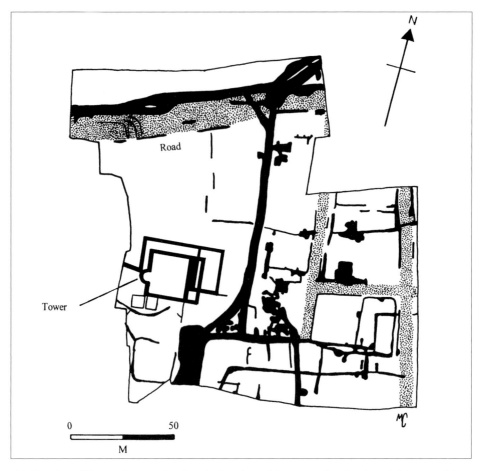

46 Site plan of Stonea Grange, showing the location of the tower that dominated this area of the Central Fens. *After Jackson and Potter, 1997. Illustration by Melanie Cameron*

being used, the type of animal remains discovered on the site, and the various botanical remains recovered) also changed when the tower was decommissioned, indicating that a very specific and 'intrusive' population was closely associated with that structure. They used different things to the people that lived in the wider settlement, and they ate different foods. We can thus envisage a small community of people from outside the area, living and working in and around the tower, bringing their tastes with them. It is probable that elsewhere they would have enjoyed better access to more 'metropolitan' culture, but serving the empire in a backwater like the Fens, they had to acquire what they could from the outside. The fact that there are only small amounts of such objects at Stonea suggests that either there was only a very small group of outsiders on the site, or, more likely (given the size of the tower), supplies in this area were limited. Who might these people have been, and what were they doing?

There are varied suggestions as to the role of this tower and its 'staff', ranging from the idea that it was the headquarters for the whole of the Fens to the approach that, large though it was, it was no more significant than a villa, or any other relatively large structure in Roman Britain, and has thus been over emphasised. The real truth may lie somewhere between these two extremes. We know that the tower cannot have been the headquarters for the whole of the Fenland landscape – the communications did not exist for it to have been so. No direct road or canal link is known to have existed between Stonea and the Silt Fens to the north. To reach areas in the Lincolnshire silts, or settlements like Spalding, the traveller would have to have left the Central Fens altogether, perhaps going as far as Durobrivae itself, before tracking north along an upland road, and then descending again into the Fens themselves. Also, it is plainly an extreme position to suggest that the site had no significance whatsoever, as Stonea was uniquely well developed for the region, and as a structure the tower would be regarded as highly unusual anywhere in the empire.

It has been suggested by the excavators, however, that this site may have been the base for a centurion who administered the surrounding area, ensuring that taxes were collected, and that the appropriate amounts of salt and salt meat were collected from the state-owned and/or private salterns functioning under licence. The centurion may also have had civic functions, ruling upon legal cases, or local disputes. It is probable that the tower functioned as a centre of this kind, though given the limitations of local communication it would have had jurisdiction over just the Central Fens, rather than the whole of the Fenland landscape. This is perhaps reinforced by a suggestion that the tower was an intrusion into the Central Fens, a symptom of the imposition of some form of exterior administration. It is possible, however, that such an imposition came not from the central authorities of the province, but from the local landowners that had an interest in the area – the villa owners from around Durobrivae. Perhaps the tower was constructed by the town, a centre to help run the industries that they had contracts with the imperial authorities to administer. A secondary function may have been to help control the new areas that were appearing as falls in sea level and more advanced drainage techniques allowed more and more land in the Fens, previously too wet to be of use, to be used for settlement and the rearing of livestock. Thus we might suggest that the tower, and the settlement around it, formed the administrative centre of this area of scattered and isolated Iron Age settlement, but which had restricted remit covering the Central Fens only.

The final site in this group that should be briefly mentioned is Flaggrass, though due to lack of excavation we have less detailed knowledge of this location than either of the others. It lies on the eastern edge of March Island, on the same island as Grandford, but on the opposite side. Flaggrass had its beginnings in the Iron Age, and when the Fen Causeway was laid out, the road appears to have diverted in its course to take in the settlement. The Fen Causeway was, however, only one communication route to run through this site, and there is evidence that

47 The A47 running across the Fens. Even today the flatness of the landscape means that many roads run dead straight for great distances – much like the Fen Causeway would once have done

Flaggrass was not only an important junction in the local canal network, but that access to the natural watercourse of the Nene was also possible from here. It is this location, at the junction of so many communication ways, that perhaps encouraged the growth and importance of the site, and made it a good location for industrial activity, particularly salt working. However, despite the 'industrial' nature of the settlement, there is still evidence of architecturally elaborate buildings – though it may be that these were related to the site's function as a junction, rather than being high-status domestic buildings. They may represent substantial warehouses, used for collecting goods and produce generated in the area, making Flaggrass an important centre for officials, and a key component in Roman control and exploitation of the area.

This situation is reminiscent of what we see in many parts of the Fenland. When we look later at the exploitation of the vast Silt Fens to the north, we shall see a well-developed Roman model for colonising and controlling such new lands. For now it is enough to say that at the heart of such new settlement was invariably a complex of tiled-roofed buildings, which possibly acted as offices and warehouses for those charged with overseeing salt production. Not only might Flaggrass have performed this function, but we see something which is possibly similar just to the north of the Central Fen islands. A small nucleus of sites in the Coldham area, including two with architectural debris in them, lie to the north of the islands, on the Silt Fens which were being opened up in the second century. Later pewter finds have also been claimed from this area. These 'richer' sites are surrounded by an area of less substantial settlement which seems to spread out around them. It is thus possible that these slightly 'richer' sites were, like their more northern counterparts (and the wealthier buildings in Flaggrass itself), the official centre from which surrounding production (principally salted meat and salt) was directed, and the location to which the produce was gathered. These sites may well have been, in effect, the heart of a supervised attempt to exploit the Fens to the north of the Central Fen islands, and to spread settlement into new areas.

The sites considered above are the most obvious manifestation of a 'Roman' presence in the Fens – that is to say the provincial and/or regional authorities. However, roads and canals also formed important elements of what we might term a 'landscape of authority', as distinct from the vast majority of settlements that we know about in the area. On most 'native' sites there is no brick, building stone, or roof tile; they were sites not in positions on Roman roads or based around the sites of Roman forts. But a landscape of authority was formed from features which overlay this landscape of relatively poor (in architectural terms) settlement. However, in that other, 'native', landscape, status was displayed through portable wealth and personal adornment in a way that harked back to the Iron Age. In this small area in the heart of the Fens we have two clear trends which are very separate: the native, with wealth expressed through objects, rather than architecture; and the infrastructure of the empire, roads, canals, and substantial buildings.

This, then, is a landscape where the imperial presence was obvious, perhaps heavy; an area too valuable because it produced salt, or too dangerous because it had, at the start of the occupation, taken part in a major revolt, to be left truly to its own devices. The people of this area continued to live in many ways much as they had always done, their own leaders signifying their rank, like their forefathers had done, through the wearing of items of personal adornment, like brooches, or bangles and torcs. But reminders that they were now part of an empire would never have been far away – the great tower brooding over the flat landscape, official traffic moving up the road or down the canals, and always the need to produce salt for the authorities, handed over to meet the obligations of taxation or rent. Those that represented that authority might not have been from too far away either, as they may have been none other than civilian officials from Durobrivae, but the scale of the changes in Fenland, especially in the last years of the first, and the first years of the second century, can have left few unaware of the power of Rome.

So, what would our traveller, in about AD 200, experience, walking down the Fen Causeway, and across this landscape? This area, as we know, used pottery that it received from the west, and our itinerant pot peddler may well have found a ready market for his goods. He has left Durobrivae by the north gate, and crossed the Nene on the bridge that carried the main road northwards. Here he turns aside into Normangate Field, and amongst the small smoke-belching kilns on the edge of the northern suburb he stocks up, buying fresh wares, newly fired pots. Then he turns east, following the road past the abandoned remains of the Longthorpe Fortress, and on towards the Fen Edge, crossing through the settlement at Fengate. This already ancient, but now declining settlement, sits on the edge of two worlds, the wet and the dry, the gate keeper to the Fens. The people who live here hunt

48 A drainage ditch in the Silt Fens. In the Roman period the Fens would quickly have become waterlogged without maintenance of the drainage ditches (very like this modern example) that criss-crossed the landscape, and the same is still true today

and fish in the marshes beyond, supplying fresh fish, fowl, and maybe objects made of Fenland resources, like baskets woven from reed, to the town a few miles away. Our traveller, however, doesn't stop here, but carries on down the road as it runs out into the 'waterland' of the Fens along a causeway of gravel, reinforced with brushwood. This road, running across unstable ground, is prone to flooding and subsidence, but it is an important highway, running east, and so considerable effort is invested in it by the authorities. The causeway has been raised several times to try and bring it above the level of the annual floodwaters, the road surface patched as it has shifted and cracked. The road doesn't run straight: it kinks and zigzags across the landscape, connecting the islands that dot the watery marshes. These islands might be only a matter of feet higher than the surrounding landscape, but that was high enough to attract settlement for hundreds of years. Now, following the Conquest, and 150 years into the occupation, these islands, supporting farms and small villages, are connected to the outside world like never before. A major east–west road runs through their quiet backwater, bringing the army, officials, and peddlers with items for sale. But the people living here are not welcoming to the outside world and, either through poverty, or an active desire to be left in peace and to live as they have always lived, they simply watch the traffic rumbling up and down this road, hoping that it will pass them by.

Beyond this island is a long, straight stretch of road passing across the Peat Fen, a lonely stretch of road, often misty and quiet. The only traffic that our peddler meets here is the occasional cart, heading the other way, out of the Fens towards the town, laden with salt, salted meat or other produce. The journey from the town is a long one, and as this stretch of road comes to an end, meeting the island of March, it is time to find somewhere to spend the night. The road runs up onto the edge of the island, and twists sharply around the site of an abandoned fort. This is the substantial settlement of Grandford, which a hundred years before had grown up round the military outpost here, and which, in a hundred years time would be being rebuilt in stone. This place, with its connections to the army, is not really a place of natives. The people who live here are the descendants of those who first moved here to serve the old fort, or those who must live and work in the area, but choose to associate themselves with the outside world – living close to the road in Roman-style houses. Many look like native dwellings from the outside, but step inside these buildings and they are painted with wall-paintings, there is glass in the windows, and fine ware pottery on the tables. It is in one of these homes that, for a price, the peddler spends the night.

Morning finds him on his way again, out of Grandford, the road continuing east to another settlement, Flaggrass, an older place with its roots in the time before the Romans. From here communication routes run in all directions, with a road and a canal running east, a canal to the south, and a road and river to the north. The road north runs into a newer settled landscape, where there are many salterns, the clouds of smoke and steam from burning fires and bubbling salt pans rising into the sky. The peddler had tried his luck in that direction before, without success. A little north of Flaggrass is the base for a minor official, a major settlement

49 Modern sea defences near the Wash coast. Such defences would probably always have been necessary to keep the sea at bay

in this new, spreading occupation, creeping across the Fen. It is the job of the official there to watch over the salterns, to ensure that salt is regularly delivered to the storehouse, so that when his superiors come, wanting the salt that is due by way of rent and taxes, there is sufficient to meet their demands. His superiors will make his life difficult if he fails, so in turn, he makes the lives of those he watches over difficult – pushing them to produce more, extracting from them more than is really due. He will force, if necessary, and once or twice he has even called in the army – a pair of soldiers came, and his demands for salt were backed by force. Few have money out there, so there is little interest in anything a peddler might bring.

Instead, our traveller turns south to follow the canal. He picks his way along the tow path, watching the large, flat-bottomed barges passing slowly by, many carrying loads of salt meat and cured hides out of the region – destined for the army, distant in the north, manning the emperor's wall. Others, travelling into the Fens, carry building materials like tile and stone. The tower of Stonea is one of the first things to come into view, visible for a great distance, a dark, square block on the horizon. The canal kinks, heading straight for the tower, and finally the peddler reaches the coast of Stonea Island. There is a wharf there, with boats loading and unloading, and the canal side path turns into a road, leading into the settlement. On the right day there would be a market here, in the market square, a market which would attract customers from all the surrounding territory, a chance to buy things from the distant town. There is no market there today, and the hard standing beneath the tower is almost empty. Two soldiers on detached duty with the centurion that governs the area from the tower, their own legion stationed far away, stand on guard at either side of the entrance. A trickle of people is always entering and leaving the building, the centre of authority here. The peddler dislikes soldiers – they can be heavy-handed, and he has experienced their rough handling many times before, but soldiers and officials have money. He approaches cautiously, engaging them in conversation, offers them small trinkets (no charge, Sir!), small bribes that ensure they turn a blind eye to him, as he accosts those coming and going, trying to sell his wares. It is hard to get pottery and other manufactured goods out here, and even when it isn't market day he can shift his stock at a profit. He knows that by midday he will have sold what he has bought, and made a reasonable amount of money. In the afternoon he will seek out a friend he has living in the village that lies around the market place. That friend usually has stuff for him – baskets, smoked fish, a little salt (sneaked away whilst the soldiers weren't looking) – and the peddler will purchase these things. After spending the night with his friend, he will make the return journey back to the town, and sell 'Fenland' produce to the townsfolk – once more, at a profit.

4

SALT FROM THE SILTS

To the north-east of Durobrivae and to the north of the Central Fens is a vast expanse of open territory termed the Lincolnshire Fens. There are two principal parts to this territory: the more coastal zone, where watercourses flowing towards the sea have deposited silt in a great bar that forms the higher and dryer 'Silt Fens', and the more inland Fens which lie behind this bar, where fresh water has pooled, encouraging the growth of peat. This more inland area, being lower, was always wetter and less habitable than the silts in the Roman period *(50);* note how few sites exist in the peat fens.

If the Central Fens, considered in Chapter Three, are a place where the Roman period occupation is characterised by a landscape which had its roots in the Iron Age, then the Lincolnshire Fens are a place where the landscape grew under the Romans *(51).* Iron Age activity in the Lincolnshire Fens appears to have been confined to seasonal occupation of salt-working sites. This is because the water levels across the Fens were higher in the late Iron Age than they were by the Roman period, and this made permanent occupation largely impossible *(52).* But not all uses of the landscape require permanent occupation, and people living on or near the Iron Age 'coast' would make their way in the summer months out into the Fenlands to areas of slightly higher ground. Silting watercourses, or isolated islands of silt, would have made ideal locations to base themselves, and, using cut peat for fuel, these seasonal salt workers would have boiled the brackish brine that backed up creeks and watercourses at high tide, to make salt. They may have subsidised this activity by hunting for fowl or fishing, both of which will have been plentiful in the Peat Fens, and the cutting of reeds might also have been a signifi-cant activity, either for the making of craft items (like baskets) to sell, or simply for use as roofing material. It may also be that, as the edges of the Fens dried out in the summer, good seasonal grazing became available – attracting people who usually occupied the uplands, droving flocks down into this pastureland. The exploitation of resources in the Fens, fish, fowl, reeds, and most importantly, salt,

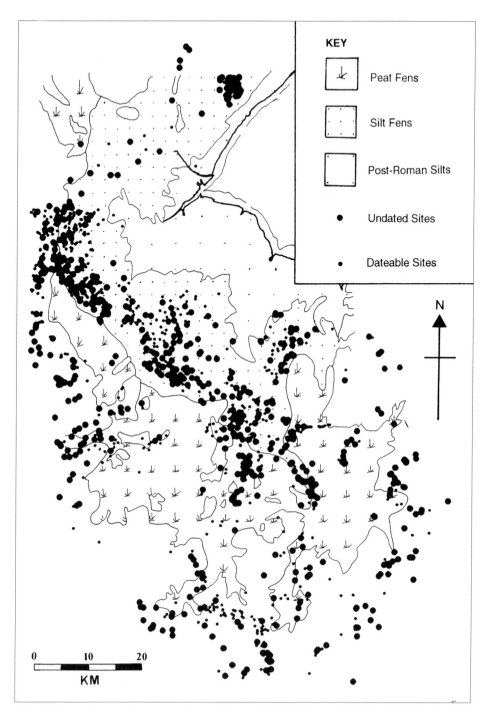

KEY

Peat Fens

Silt Fens

Post-Roman Silts

● Undated Sites

● Dateable Sites

N

0   10   20
KM

50 A map showing the sites that cannot be dated to a specific century. This shows how many sites we know too little about to fit them into our chronological picture – and illustrates how high a degree of uncertainty exists around our understanding of how the Fens developed

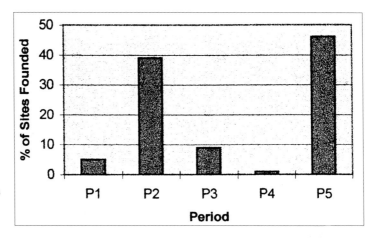

51 Graph showing the number of sites founded in the Silt Fens only in each century of the Roman occupation. Note the high number of sites founded in period two, the second century, the great era of expanding settlement in the Fens

may thus have been implemented by people who were seasonally mobile, and who were taking advantage of other opportunities, like salt making, as they became available. This activity would have been on a small scale, as we know of only limited numbers of sites in the Silt Fens occupied in the Iron Age, and when the winter closed in, the salt makers would have left, returning to higher ground.

The salt industry in this area would only have been viable if there were a centre through which the salt could be sold, (as was the case in the Roman period when Durobrivae seems to have functioned as the salters' market). But Durobrivae was founded only in the second century, so where was its Iron Age predecessor? The answer can never be known for sure, but the most likely candidate must be the major Corieltauvian site of Old Sleaford. Evidence for the site is fragmentary, but we do know that even before the Conquest those that lived here were importing small quantities of goods such as wine and olive oil (fragments of the containers of such produce, amphorae, have been found here), suggesting that it acted as a centre for trade. We also know that it was a centre for the minting of silver coinage. This indicates that in addition to its economic significance, it may also have had a high degree of political importance. The site declined in the Roman period, never developing into a true urban centre, but in the decades before the Conquest it had reached a level of some sophistication. This, combined with its position some four miles from the edge of the Fens in the Iron Age, make it the most promising candidate as a 'gateway' site to the Fens, the place to where all goods (salt, fish, fowl, reeds and reed work) from the Fens would have been channelled. It may have been, for example, that people living down the Fen Edge made their living by seasonal exploitation of the Fens. This would have entailed a semi-nomadic existence, moving their flocks from upland to Fen Edge, making salt and hunting during the summer months, but moving back to the upland to sell their sheep and other produce in the winter, through a market at Old Sleaford. However, by the time of the Roman occupation, circumstances were beginning to change *(53)*. The Silt Fens, possibly through a combination of falling sea levels, and a rising of

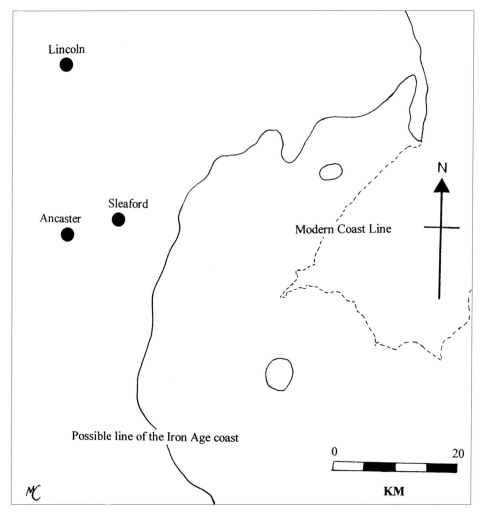

Lincoln

Sleaford

Ancaster

Modern Coast Line

N

Possible line of the Iron Age coast

0   20

KM

52 A map showing the Iron Age coast in the Wash area around the year 200 BC. Note how far inland from the modern coast the Iron Age coast ran, and how close Sleaford was to the coast at this time. *After Simmons, 1980. Illustration by Melanie Cameron*

the level of the ground (as more silt was deposited), were becoming drier, and where the low-lying and wetter peat ended, and the slightly raised bar of silt that lay between the freshwater peat and the sea began, it became possible to live.

We have a great deal of information for the Roman period in this area. Firstly, there is a vast expanse of crop marks. Crop marks are formed because modern crops are affected in their growth by the archaeology which lies beneath them. An ancient ditch, filled with loose soil, will trap moisture, and crops growing above such a feature will become taller than those elsewhere. Solid remains, like, for example, the foundation of a wall, will have the opposite effect, stunting the growth of crops above – they will be shorter than normal. These differences can be observed from the air, and over time a rich picture of field boundaries, drove

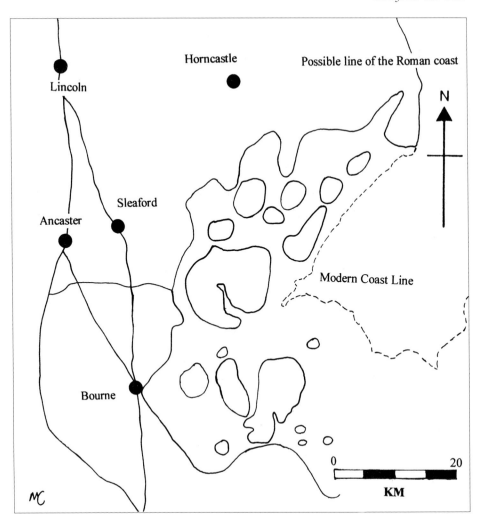

Lincoln

Horncastle

Possible line of the Roman coast

N

Sleaford

Ancaster

Modern Coast Line

Bourne

0   20

KM

MC

53 The Roman coast in the Wash area around the year AD 200. This illustrates areas of the Fens that may have been stable enough for occupation. *After Simmons, 1980. Illustration by Melanie Cameron*

ways, walls, and other such features can be built up. In the case of Roman Fenland, we have not a few fields, or an occasional building outline, but an enormous expanse of crop marks stretching right across the Silt Fens, revealing ancient water-courses, field systems, roads, and small enclosures that would once have surrounded buildings. This provides a source of information about the layout of the landscape in the Roman period unrivalled by any other location in Britain, and has been the focus of three major studies since the 1970s *(54)*.

If we can see so much, what do we know about the development of the landscape here? Occupation spread rapidly in the latter years of the first and the early years of the second century, and we can see clearly in the way that sites spread, fanning out from these earlier areas of occupation, that the areas which

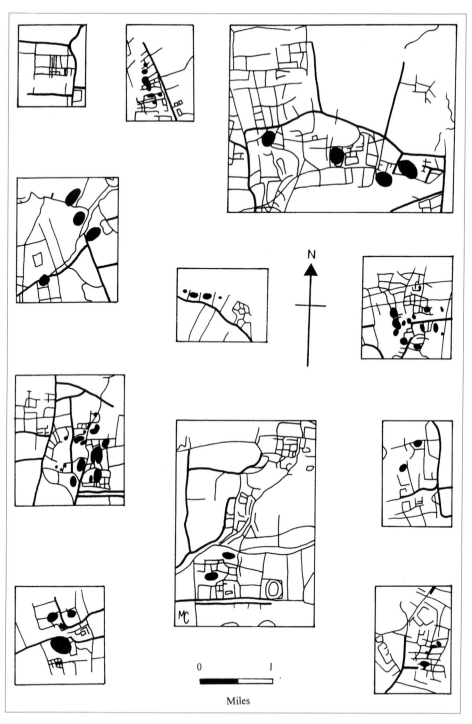

54 Settlements and drove ways on the Silt Fens, seen in the crop marks. *After Phillips, 1970.*
Illustration by Melanie Cameron

55 A modern track on the Silt Fens illustrates what a Roman drove way would have looked like, with an earthen pathway between two ditches

were inhabited in the Iron Age acted as the 'nuclei' of the later Roman settlement. The spread of sites appears to be so swift that it has often been suggested that it occurred as a direct result of the Roman authorities deliberately settling people in the area. However, we must bear in mind that our ability to date these sites accurately rests upon small numbers of pottery fragments, and when trying to establish when a site was first occupied we can probably only be accurate to within about half a century (for example, a date might fall between AD 200 and 250). So, although the speed of occupation was certainly dramatic, it may not have been instantaneous, given the difficulties in dating sites precisely, and the increase in sites across the Fens might perhaps have been over two generations. On this less dramatic timescale, the spread of occupation may have occurred simply as a result of new opportunities opening up as new land became available, and through the natural rise in population numbers. As we see a rise in the number of sites (and therefore the population) in the Silt Fens, we also see the spread of field systems and interconnecting drove ways – green lanes with ditches either side of them, used for driving (or 'droving') livestock from place to place *(55)*. 'Roddons', natural waterways which had silted up by the time of the Roman occupation, were more stable than the landscape around them. Formed of compacted silt, they were the focus for these spreading settlements, particularly in areas of otherwise unstable and shifting Fen.

An important feature of the landscape which must also be considered is the Car Dyke, not least because of the arguments which surround its function *(56)*. These different theories are informative in showing us how different scholars have

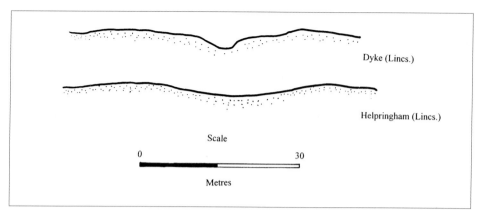

Dyke (Lincs.)

Helpringham (Lincs.)

Scale

0   30

Metres

56 A section through the Car Dyke. *After Todd, 1973*

interpreted the Fens, and in particular the Silt Fens in Lincolnshire. The dyke is a linear earthwork, running north–south along most of the western edge of the Fens, from Cambridge to the vicinity of Lincoln. It has been suggested since the earliest scholarship regarding the area that it was a military canal. The theory, forwarded by the antiquarian Stukeley in the eighteenth century, was that the Fenland was producing wheat for the army in the north, which was manning Hadrian's Wall. The grain would have been collected as sharecroppers' rent, and was then, according to Stukeley's theory, shipped north via the Car Dyke, then continuing via the coast to the wall. This idea, the Car Dyke as a transport way, was still current in the 1970s when *Fenland in Roman Times*, a large volume of survey information, was published by the Royal Geographical Society, with the variation that what was being shipped was beef and leather, rather than grain. This made sense – grain would not really have grown in the salty marsh, and the production of beef (cattle being raised in the fields of the field system noted through crop marks) alongside salt production suggests that the cattle were slaughtered, butchered, and the meat preserved for transport by salting.

The difficulty with this theory, which elegantly fits the broad facts, is that the canal is not continuous. It is formed of various sections with breaks between them. Neither is it on a level, which is essential for a canal if the water in it is not to drain away. This has led to two other theories about the dyke. The first is that it was a giant 'catch water', a drain designed to intercept rain water which had fallen on the higher ground to the west, and which might have run down into the Fens and overwhelmed the drainage system. The water would have been held in the catch water and 'flushed' into the Wash at low tide. This is an interesting suggestion, but it too has its difficulties. The problem with this theory is that it requires many people to man the system, and of this there is little evidence.

A final suggestion is that the dyke was principally a demarcation line. The dyke, in this theory, was effectively a trench cut across land to separate two different parts of the landscape, the area to the west belonging to the civil authority of the province, and the area to the east, so the theory goes, a great imperial estate. If the Car Dyke were to be seen as such a dividing line, it would also mean that the whole of the Fens was distanced from the town and administered directly for the emperor. The principal arguments for the Fens being a single imperial position have been considered in detail in Chapter Three, and have been found to be largely unconvincing. This makes the identification of the Car Dyke as a political boundary between imperial and non-imperial land unlikely.

What then was the Car Dyke? This, without clear evidence, is not a question that can be definitively solved. However, it is likely that it performed more than one function. Its positioning on the edge of the Fens, thus acting as the boundary between the two different types of landscape, upland and fen, cannot be accidental. Perhaps it marks the edge of 'useful land', the boundary between farmland to the west and the dangerous marshes to the east. It does also seem, despite its discontinuous nature, to function as a transport way, suggested by the fact that settlement concentrates along it, and is particularly dense at junctions with more minor canals running east–west into the Fens, or roads, similarly orientated. This is not a difficulty if considered locally, rather than as an attempt, for example, to join Cambridge with York. Individual stretches of it might have proved useful as short canals, allowing local traders to transport their goods easily between the various settlements that clustered on the Fen Edge. Perhaps it also performed a role as a catch water, intercepting run off, possibly not as complex a system as has sometimes been envisaged, but a mechanism to halt the worst of the rainwater that otherwise might flood the Fens, with east–west channels being a crude

57 A modern road in the Fens. Note how it is higher than the field next to it. The 'banking' of roads, to help keep them above the level of possible floodwater, is known from Roman roads in the area, like the Fen Causeway

attempt to funnel the water intercepted out towards the Wash. The Car Dyke may well have been all of the things that it has been suggested to be, but none of them in entirety.

Having reconsidered traditional views of the region, can we begin to say anything positive about what we do understand? One key aspect of the Fens that we can be certain of is that the area had firm connections to the town of Durobrivae. This much is obvious in the structure of local communications. Canals and roads reach eastwards into the Fens from either the Car Dyke or King Street, which runs parallel to it, a little to the west. These roads and canals do not run to the east side of the Fens – they halt in the Fens. For people living on the Lincolnshire silts these communication ways represent the only form of contact with the outside world, with the single exception of natural watercourses running into the Wash, which provided them with access to the sea. The principal road that anyone leaving the Fens would have encountered first would have been King Street, running north–south. To the north it runs to Old Sleaford, as we have suggested, the old market place for the salters in the late Iron Age, but in the Roman period the road also runs south to the much more important centre of Durobrivae.

If we can say that the silts were controlled from Durobrivae, what of the actual settlements out in the Fenland landscape? At first glance the sites which spread out across the Silt Fens appear to be an undifferentiated expanse of farms. However, careful analysis of the landscape, both in terms of its geographical structure and its development over time, indicate that this was not the case. Indeed its development throws interesting light upon what was actually happening in the area during the Roman occupation.

First, let us examine the crop marks. One of the most important things to recognise about them is that they come in two distinct types. First, there are the clearly artificial ones, the straight sides of fields, the long parallel marks of drove ways, or the small enclosures which probably surrounded buildings *(58)*. These are all artefacts of an artificial, man-made landscape, and give us a good indication of where people were living and working. The second type of crop mark is that of the natural, irregular watercourse. Here are the relics of small brooks and streams that ran through the Silt Fen where it had not been tamed and ordered by people. The crucial thing about this is the relationship between the two types of crop marks. The artificial and regular crop marks do not stretch in a continuous band across the landscape – they are discontinuous, arranged in five distinct 'clumps', each clump with a gap between it and the next. These gaps are not simply areas where we have failed to collect information, because there is information from these gaps. It is precisely here that we see the irregular and natural crop marks of ancient streams. What this indicates is that, at its fullest and most developed, the landscape of the Silt Fens was made up of five distinct areas of settlement (let's call these 'Fenland Communities'), with buildings, fields and drove ways, but that between these five areas of occupation there remained areas of untamed Fen, full

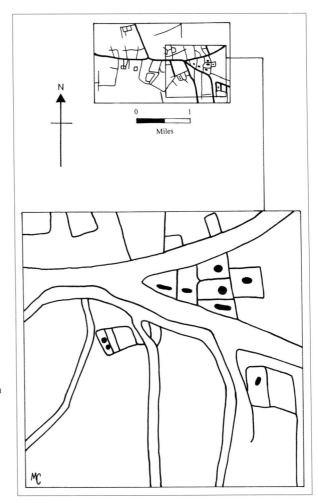

58 Detail of a small hamlet from the Silt Fens, seen in the crop marks. The dark blotches are areas of debris that mark the site of buildings. Note how each building is enclosed in its own small compound, and how the drove ways are clearly visible running through the settlement. *After Phillips, 1970 and Simmons, 1980. Illustration by Melanie Cameron*

of creeks and streams *(59)*. This has two implications for any consideration of communications into and across the Fens. Initially, we must note that the principal communication ways discussed above, the east–west canals and roads that connect either with the Car Dyke or King Street, occurred at intervals. Each one of the channels/roads that run east in this way connects with a clump of settlement. Most of these communities are served by one such connection to the outside world, though occasionally a community is served by two. This becomes more significant when we consider communication between communities.

Within each area of field system there are drove ways, small lanes which connect the settlements to the fields and to each other. However, it's crucial to note that the droves do not cross the areas of natural watercourses. In other words the droves do not run from community to community. The crop marks suggest that there was actually no way of travelling between the communities 'laterally', and that they were, to all intents and purposes, isolated from each other. The only

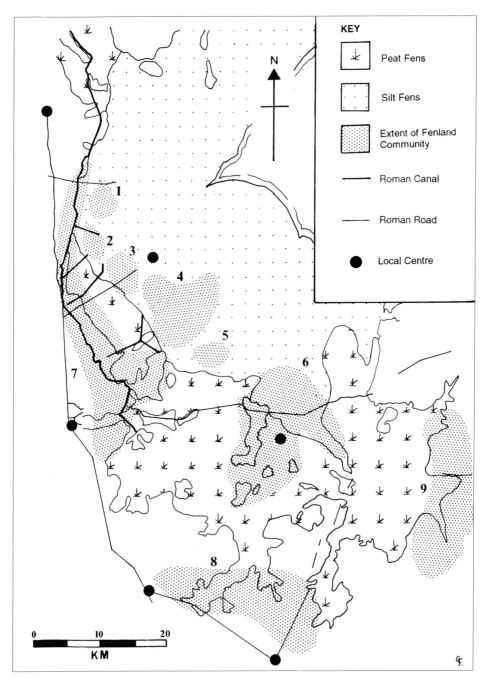

KEY

☒ Peat Fens

☒ Silt Fens

☒ Extent of Fenland
Community

—— Roman Canal

—— Roman Road

● Local Centre

N

1
2
3
4
5
6
7
8
9

0   10   20
KM

59 A map of the Fenland area, showing the different Fenland communities, on the Silt Fens, the Central Fens, and the Fen Edge

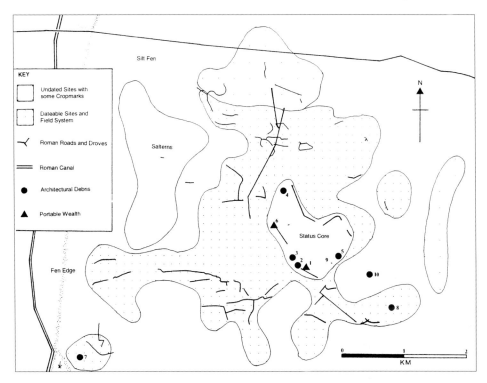

60 A map of community one (the general location of which is shown on 58). Note the status core, surrounded by the field system. On the edge of this area of occupation are the salterns

way of moving from one to the other would be to leave the Fens entirely, by moving up the east–west connecting road or canal to the upland, then following the north–south communications route (King Street or the Car Dyke), reaching the next east–west route, and then heading back into the Fens. As we shall see, this aspect of the physical layout of the Fenland landscape is important to how we interpret what was happening here.

The communities themselves are not, however, simple and undifferentiated areas internally – within each there is structure. We can be sure that this structure is real, as it is repeated to varying degrees in each of the five communities; for example the system of drove ways is not random. At the heart of each community is a ring of droves, about one mile in diameter. From this 'central ring-road' droves radiate in spokes, out into the field system. Smaller droves run off the 'spokes', connecting outlying fields and settlements. The communications routes from the outside world all connect either directly with the central ring or with a spoke which runs into it. This skeleton of droves seems to act as a framework for both the field system and the distribution of settlements, with buildings and fields clustering around the spokes and the ring-road. But this is not the only sense of structure apparent – there is also structure in the type of sites in these communities, and where within each community they occur.

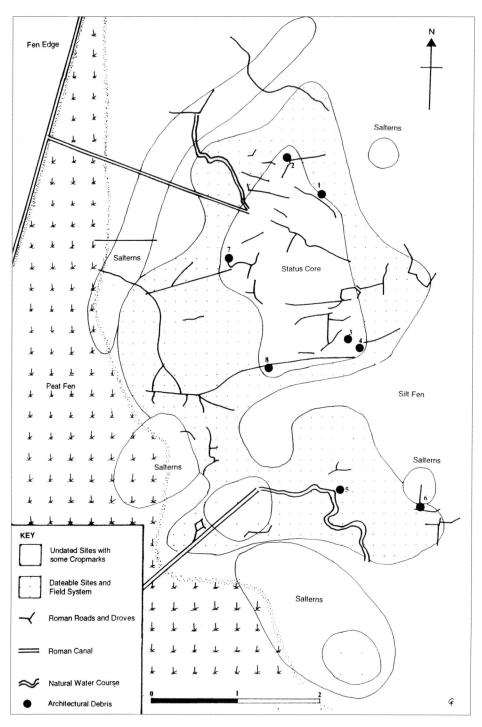

Fen Edge

Salterns

N

Salterns

2

1

7

Status Core

3
4

8

Peat Fen

Silt Fen

Salterns

Salterns

5

6

KEY

Undated Sites with
some Cropmarks

Dateable Sites and
Field System

Roman Roads and Droves

Roman Canal

Natural Water Course

Architectural Debris

Salterns

0   1   2

G

61 A map of community two (the general location of which is shown on 59)

When we are considering 'site types' in the Fenland landscape, we must think carefully about what kind of evidence we are using. The Fens have, as discussed earlier, been intensively surveyed. Thus, most of the information that we have about sites is of this kind, but survey data has both strengths and limitations. The first point to note is that a survey is a method of gaining an overview of the landscape. It involves walking over ploughed ground, and collecting any visible debris that has been pulled to the surface. This gives a good idea of where sites are, but not what they were like, and as a study it aims to establish presence or absence. What is actually picked up during fieldwalking, normally metal work, pottery sherds, tile and brick, is significant in terms of considering the nature of the site, but only insofar as it might give an indication that a certain type of pottery was used, or that a structure had, for example, a tiled roof. This kind of information, however, cannot begin to give us the kind of detail that an excavation would, so for the bulk of sites out in the Fens we have no sense of ground plan, or development over time. We just have a sense of what was present or absent, and some crude sense of when the site was occupied. This is indicated by the pottery present, which can be loosely dated to a particular century. In considering settlement types in this kind of situation, then, it is not appropriate to attempt to understand sites through ground plans, as has been done with villas. A rather looser categorisation based upon the kind of material discovered during the survey is a more productive approach. A recent study (*Landscapes of Imperialism: Roman and Native Interaction in the East Anglian Fenland*) did precisely this, adopting a three-fold division of sites by broad type, based upon the kind of evidence recovered. These three types were: sites with no fine ware; sites with fine ware but no other signs of wealth; and sites with signs of wealth interpreted in a broad sense (including any indication of substantial architecture, like roof tile, brick or stone, and more portable forms of wealth like jewellery, coins, etc.). This simple categorisation is the one adopted here.

What happens, then, when the sites within a community are looked at in this fashion? The result is a clear division of where, within each community, those kinds of sites lie *(63)*. The bulk of sites showing some sign of wealth lie in the centre of the communities, around the inner ring of droves that we have already identified in considering communications. Some thirty-one of these sites (out of forty-four) are of the type where substantial architecture has been discovered, i.e. tile and brick. There were, in fact, only thirteen sites in the whole of the Silt Fens where any sign of portable wealth has been found. This tells us that the bulk of wealth in the region was of the more traditionally Roman form of 'architectural elaboration', that buildings were being consciously made of Roman materials in a Roman style – as opposed to signs of personal wealth like coins and metal work considered from the Central Fens in the last chapter. Thus wealth, of whatever kind, was clearly concentrated in the centre of these communities.

We can explore this nature of 'wealth' a little further, and the instance of wealthy sites can be mapped *(64)*. The structures that we are considering would mostly have tiled roofs. In the previous chapter we looked at the Central Fens, and established that there is an identifiable architectural tradition in the region, using local building materials. As this entailed thatched roves, and daub or cob walls, all fairly flexible and forgiving materials, there was no requirement for perfectly squared buildings. Once a tiled roof was introduced, however, the situation changed radically. To fit a tiled roof to a structure the walls must be regular to carry the evenly sawn timbers required to make the framework that tiles need to rest upon. The presence of tile, therefore, although a material confined to the roof of a structure, has implications for the whole style of building, and it indicates a style alien to the Fens. This suggests that these few structures, at the heart of the Silt Fen communities, are an implant, an insertion from outside, somewhat in the manner of the 'official' landscape identified in the Central Fens. They in no way represent a development of, or anything that may be related to, the native tradition of architecture from the Fens in this period. We are not seeing traditional Fenland buildings which had simply been enhanced with the addition of a tiled roof, but structures which were entirely different from what had gone before.

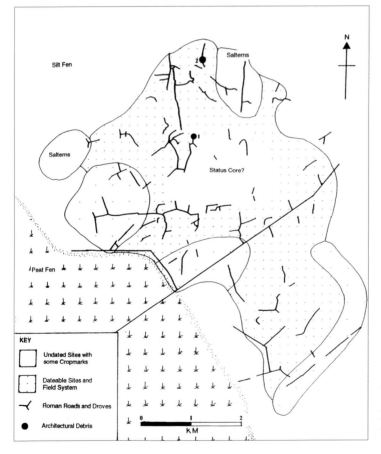

62 A map of community three (the general location of which is shown on 59)

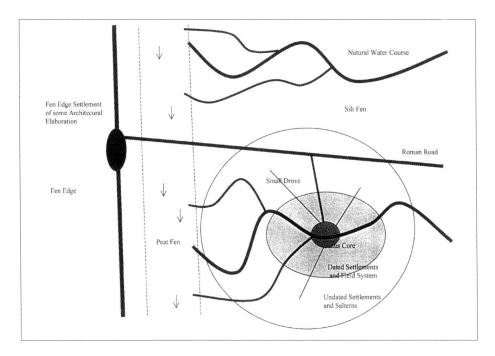

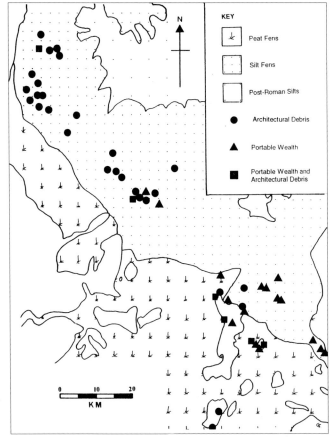

63 Above A 'schematic' model of a Silt Fen community, showing the basic features that are common to them all. The model shows the status core – where the key buildings of high status (i.e. those with tiled roofs) are located, surrounded by the field system, and finally the undated sites and salterns. Note also the Fen Edge settlement, linked to the Silt Fen community. This is the possible location of minor officials involved in controlling the salt-production industry

64 Right A map showing the distribution of different kinds of wealth in the Silt and Central Fens. Note the different clusters of wealth in the Silt Fens – these are the status cores of the different Silt Fen communities

A further point that we can make about these structures concerns the number of them, relative to the number of sites in each community. If we were looking at an elite group, growing naturally out of the local population, we would expect to see such sites comprising a relatively constant proportion of sites in each community. The communities are of different sizes, ranging from 115 to twenty-three sites. The bigger the community, the more sites of this type we would expect to see, as more people in bigger communities would have the required wealth to indulge in such building. This is not, however, the pattern that emerges. There are always around six such sites, located at the heart of each community, no matter what its size. This suggests that this group of sites performed a fixed function within each community, a function which required six such structures, no matter how big or small the community became. An obvious function for such sites, being in all cases amongst the best-connected sites to the outside world, would be something like an 'administration' centre, a base for officials operating in the area. Given the fact that we have already identified them as belonging to a style of archi-tecture which properly belongs outside the Fens, the idea that they form some kind of official complex at the heart of each community seems even more likely.

The second type of settlement within the Silt Fen communities that we need to consider is that of the fine ware using site *(67 and 68)*. These sites are inter-esting, both because they fit into a specific location within our growing model of a Silt Fen community, and because it is generally fine ware pottery that we can date: it is these sites which provide us with information on the way in which this landscape developed over time. The first thing to note about such sites is that they form a rough band, surrounding the 'core' of higher-status sites. They are generally located where there are obvious indications that the landscape has been 'tamed', that is where crop marks show fields and drove ways. They are often clustered around, or close to, the principal drove ways radiating out from the community's central area. The close connection between these sites and the field system suggests that they are probably small farms, the occupants of which would have made a home in the Fens, and made a living by farming cattle or sheep.

This leaves a third group of sites, those which did not use fine ware pottery. Like the first two groups, this third group also exists in a specific location within the 'community' structure. These sites are concentrated around the edges of the communities, beyond the areas of crop marks and datable settlements. Many of them are also associated with briquetage – the ceramic fragments left behind by the salt-making process. Brine, or salty water, was collected in receptacles, often large, square, tray-like objects made of rough ceramic. These trays were supported upon ceramic columns, allowing a fire to be lit beneath them. The heat from below would evaporate the water, leaving a solid 'cake' of salt in the container. The fragments of ceramic from broken columns and containers are the most archaeo-logically detectable trace of the salt-making process, and often occur in large quan-tities on these 'fringe' sites, suggesting that these locations were part of the salt-making industry *(69)*. Salt production is an unpleasant process, generating a lot

65 Right A reconstructed *tegula* roof tile. The upturned lip at the edge would have been pressed hard against the lip of the neighbouring tile and the join between the two covered with an *imbrex* (66)

66 Below The curved *imbrex* covers the gap between neighbouring flat tiles, or *tegulae*

67 Above Samian pottery.
Along with Nene Valley ware
colour coat (see *27*), Samian
is the most common fine ware
found in the Fens

68 Left Fine ware (like this
Samian) is often found in
large quantities on sites, and
allows settlements to be dated.
The presence of Samian
generally indicates occupation
during the first and second
centuries. *Photograph by Gillian
Hawkes*

of smoke and steam, and it makes sense that salt-production sites should be located at the edge of the settled area, as far away from the occupied farms as practically possible. Salt is usually only made in the summer months, and so, as with their Iron Age predecessors, we can postulate that sites close to the saltworks were occupied perhaps only seasonally, during the salt-making period. This would explain their generally insubstantial nature, with no evidence of developed architecture, or even much sign of ceramics. If they were occupied for only a few months of the year it seems logical that the inhabitants would ether take their pottery with them when they left, or perhaps never even take it at all. They may have simply made do without, perhaps using wooden vessels which would leave little or no trace in the archaeological record, whilst they were working in the salterns.

To summarise, the Fens seem to have been divided into distinct areas, each with a central core, in which there were around six sites, probably arranged around a circular drove way, and acting as an administrative centre. Around this core was a system of fields and drove ways, populated with small farms, many of which would have used fine ware pottery. This area was probably used for stockrearing. Finally, there was a zone of relatively insubstantial sites that were probably only seasonally occupied, and which were connected with salt production.

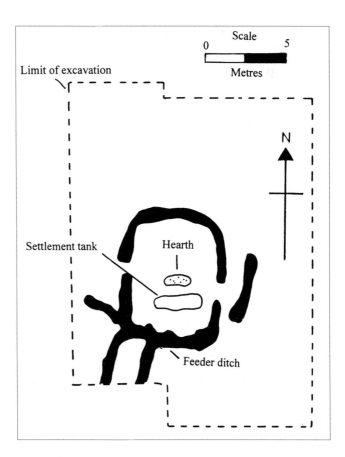

69 Plan of a Fenland saltern. *After Leah, 1992*

If we now understand something of the structure of these communities, what can we say about how the different elements, the high-status centre, farmland and farms, and salterns were interrelated to each other? This is a complex question, but a situation of a similar nature to this has been studied elsewhere, specifically on the south coast by Richard Bradley. When looking at the south coast, it became clear to Bradley that salt production cannot have been a full-time occupation. It was seasonal, occurring largely in the months from May to September, when the weather was dry enough to allow the salt to be easily evaporated over open fires. Being seasonal, salt production has to be a supplement to some other activity – it would not provide someone with an income all year round. We can suggest, then, that the salt makers of the Fens worked to a similar calendar as the one proposed by Bradley for the south coast. In the Fens it can be suggested that the same people who were farming the field systems were also engaged in salt production as an 'added extra' to their farming. But we can go a little further that this. Salt was important in the ancient world because it was one of the methods used for preserving meat (the others being smoking or curing). This offers us a possible link with the field systems. If the ground was too salty to grow crops, the fields must have been used for stockrearing. Once the animals raised in these fields were slaughtered, the meat would have to be either salted or smoked, and given the salt-making industry in the area, salted meat is the probable end product of the field/saltern system we can see in the Fens. If, as suggested earlier, the sites around the ring drove in the centre of the communities performed some sort of administrative function, we might suggest that their purpose was to administer the production of salt, salted meat and perhaps meat on the hoof.

Although not located in the Fens, there is a fourth layer of settlement, which adds the final element to the Silt Fen communities. At, or close to, the junction of each east–west communication ways into the Fens with the north–south routes of the Car Dyke and King Street, we find large complexes of sites *(70)*. These are usually well appointed in terms of their architecture, thus clearly linking them in style to the structures in each community around the central ring of drove ways, rather than the actual farms themselves. Occupation along the Fen Edge clusters noticeably at these points, and so such settlements are not random concentrations of population. They are, in fact, positioned in such a way that anyone or anything leaving the Silt Fens would have to pass through them – as would any produce leaving for Durobrivae. In terms of the organisation of this area it is conceivable that these are the next step up from the sites in the heart of each community, part of the 'chain of command' that controlled the salt-production process. As such, these settlements might be considered the bases of officials working for those holding the contract from the imperial authorities for the extraction of salt. If this were the case, such officials are likely to have been given responsibility for the extraction of sufficient salt and salted meat to fulfil that contract, plus sufficient extra to provide a profit. This, of course, leaves us with the question of who actually held the contract to supply salt, and who was ultimately in charge of the

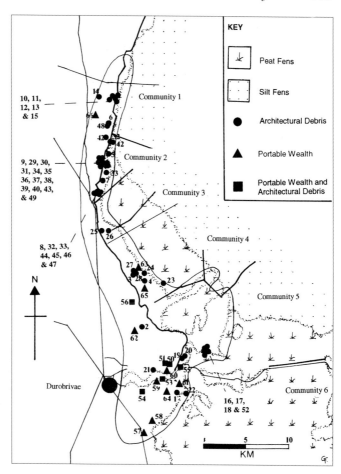

70 Map showing the distribution of substantial Roman settlements on the Fen Edge. Note how the sites cluster on, or close to, the ends of roads and canals running into the Fens

salt industry? This can only be answered 'in the round' by looking at other parts of the hinterland of Durobrivae, and is a subject to which we shall return in later chapters.

However, we can address another question which is still unanswered: where did the produce of this area, salted meat, possibly leather, and salt itself, go? A clue to this lies in the only element of the Silt Fen landscape that we have so far not considered, that of Spalding. Spalding is a settlement about which we know little, with the exception that there was a considerable concentration of wealth there. It was, however, clearly more developed than the average Fenland farming settlement. We also know that it lay at a hub of communication, with several of the east–west communications routes from the upland running right through the communities that they connect to, and ending at Spalding. In addition to this, in Roman times, Spalding lay at the end of a long inlet from the Wash – it had access to the sea, and so was probably a small port. We know too little about this possible port at Spalding to be sure about its relationship to the Fens, but we can make a suggestion, a theory which grows out of the suggestions of Dugdale and Stukeley (writing in 1772 and 1776 respectively). It was suggested by them, as noted earlier, that the Fens were great expanses put under production to feed the army stationed on Hadrian's Wall, though as we have seen, the details of this theory, that the Fenland population were set to work growing grain that was shipped north via the Car Dyke, were inaccurate. The army did need meat and salt, however, and consumed one of the by-products of raising cattle (leather) in great quantity, using it for everything from tents to armour. It is possible that the 'contract' that we have talked about, which gave local elites the power to work the salt industry in the emperor's name, was actually tied to army supply. The contract probably involved payment in kind: those running the contract handing over produce directly to the authorities in exchange for the right to run the salt-production industry. The surplus generated for the benefit of those who ran the salt works (the profit for those that held the contract) would have been moved west, ultimately ending up at Durobrivae, but what of the payment required under the contract? That payment in kind might have been for military use, say, perhaps, a set amount of salt, salted meat and leather to be delivered to the army. If such goods could not be shipped via the Car Dyke, perhaps they were shipped by sea, up the east coast, with ships loading at Spalding before sailing north for Hadrian's Wall. A concrete link between the Durobrivae area and Hadrian's Wall exists, with large quantities of Nene Valley pottery, produced just to the west of the town, found all along the wall, suggesting a well-established trade between the two.

What does this tell us about the organisation of the salt-production industry? If we accept that Durobrivae was the market centre for the production of salt during the Roman period, but also that production of salt was farmed out to the local aristocracy, we should look for evidence of such a ruling class – and, when we look, there is indeed evidence for them. The landscape to the west of Durobrivae offers an important clue to who these people might have been, for here we encounter the large villas of the Nene Valley *(25)*. The individuals that owned these residences were also those who, in all probability, exercised power over the town, being members of the ruling council of Durobrivae. It is this elite that may also have been responsible for the salt making in the Central Fens, and the building of the stone tower at Stonea. It thus seems probable that salt production in the Silt Fens would also have come under their control.

Thus we have a fairly good understanding of the structure of the landscape, how it was controlled, and what was produced. What we have not, so far, considered, is what it would have been like to actually live in the Silt Fens. Richard Hingley, in examining the layout of similar landscapes in other regions that exhibit what is called a 'girdle pattern', has suggested that they have strong links to Iron Age 'kinship'. These types of settlement can be seen in the way that Roman period occupation was laid out in the Thames Valley and Wetwang Slack in Yorkshire. Hingley suggests that areas of ground would be enclosed in a central ring of droves, and that this land would be held in common by a kinship group (a large extended family). Rather than inheriting the farm of the parents, children would build their own home and claim a stake in the use of the communal land. Thus, as the population increased, this settlement pattern would spread, but sites would not stay in occupation for long periods of time, a generation at most. Old farms would thus be abandoned, and would fall out of use. However, Hingley also identifies this pattern in the settlements of the Silt Fens *(71)*, with the physical layout of settlements around open areas of what may have been communal land, but also a rapid turnover of the occupation of settlements. We see many sites failing, but also many being created in a constant process of site failure and foundation. What this suggests is that the people who moved out into the Fens may well have preserved their pre-Roman social structure, which shows an essentially Iron Age pattern of settlement based upon kinship. The landscape of the Silt Fens, then, like that of the Central Fens, is an Iron Age one (even if 'transplanted' from elsewhere). However, as already explored through our consideration of tiled buildings, this was a situation in which an external group had, in effect, come to dominate the local population.

There is something else that we might note about the layout of the landscape that gives us another clue about the lives that people lived here. As considered earlier, communication between these communities was impossible without leaving the Fens, but even such an activity would have been difficult. Peasants in pre-modern agricultural societies, dependent upon their own labour to survive and be fed, will rarely travel more than four miles from home. Four miles there and four back is effectively the distance that can be travelled on foot in a day – a limit because to stay anywhere overnight is too expensive, and entails too great a loss of time. The distance needed to travel to a neighbouring community, via the upland, would thus be prohibitive. A journey from, for example, community one, to its southern neighbour, community two, would have been about seven miles, and the journey to Durobrivae itself would have taken even longer *(73)*. This means two things: firstly, that the inhabitants of the Fens are unlikely to have had much inclination to travel casually, and may not have had much contact with neighbouring communities, but also that their access to manufactured goods (like pottery) would have been strictly limited.

If the nearest identifiable trading centre where manufactured goods might have been acquired, Durobrivae, would have been too far away to visit regularly, we need to explain how such large quantities of such goods (particularly pottery) are present in the Fens. If it is unlikely that these people will have left the Fens to acquire them, then the goods must have come to the Fens. A model for this is the *nundinae*, or 'nine-day market', known from other areas of the empire where markets travelled around a given area, setting up in different places on a nine-day cycle. It is also known from Africa that large estates controlled the access of the estate workers to the outside world by holding specially sanctioned markets on the grounds, allowing tenants to meet their needs without travelling. The landscape in the Fens is thus very controlling – the population of the Fens was located in places where it had very little ability to travel, little access to the local market centre, and

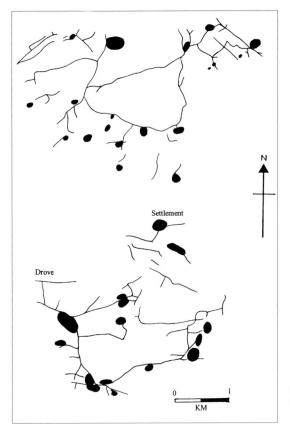

71 Examples of girdle pattern settlements on the Silt Fens identified from the crop marks. *After Hingley, 1989. Illustration by Melanie Cameron*

any access to such goods as it did have is likely to have been through travelling markets which, for reasons which we shall explore later when we consider the nature of economic relations between different parts of the Durobrivae hinterland, were probably also closely controlled.

The inhabitants of the area were living and working in the Fens to conduct an unpleasant task, salt working, in an isolated environment, and were probably under close supervision by authorities running the salt production. The reasons behind such a draconian landscape are difficult to understand, but the fact, already noted, that salt was a valuable commodity in the ancient world, and that it was probably being produced under licence from the imperial authorities, may provide the answer. Producing something valuable in large quantities in an open landscape may have led to theft, fraud and loss of profits – ensuring that the salt-production areas were relatively secure may have been a way to counter these risks, but the resulting landscape would not have been a pleasant or easy place in which to live.

We should now rejoin our traveller, who has returned to Durobrivae from the Central Fens and is heading north. What does he experience? If he were travelling up King Street, perhaps with pottery of the Nene Valley industry acquired at a market in Durobrivae itself, he might well be heading for one of the estate markets out in a Fenland community. Leaving the town from the north, he must first cross the river, passing the site of the abandoned fort that had once guarded the crossing. He quickly reaches a well-established bridge, carrying Ermine Street across the Nene, the river narrow and flowing fast at this point. Across the river, he passes through the industrial suburb in the Normangate Field area, small buildings crowding close to the road, but beyond them, glimpsed through gaps in the frontage, is the 'industrial' area, with pottery kilns and iron ore smelting pits sending columns of smoke into the sky – the same smoke glimpsed from the south, as our traveller had first approached the town. This suburb quickly peters out and, taking a right fork off Ermine Street, the traveller soon finds himself on the edge of the upland, the ground sloping down sharply at his right-hand side. The Car Dyke, a long, straight canal of still water, is located between him and the start of a flat expanse of wet peat that stretches away to the east. Reeds and perhaps alder are growing thickly as the freshwater marshes deepen.

Some way to the north our traveller comes across the first 'bailiff's house', a complex of buildings sitting upon the junction between King Street and an east–west road running out into the Fens. This building appears wellappointed, of stone construction, tiled roof, perhaps also with warehouses for storing produce. How closely controlled were the Fenland farmers? As we have suggested above, the very layout of the landscape appears to be controlling, but we should not make the mistake of thinking the Roman authorities were the only people able to act harshly. With money at stake, local elites seem likely culprits for the harsh oppression hinted at in the way that these Fenland communities were organised. If so, it

72 Waterways would have been crucial to life in Fenland during the Roman period, running through settlements and being used as routes for travel and trade. The same is true of today's Fenland, with embanked waterways running through villages

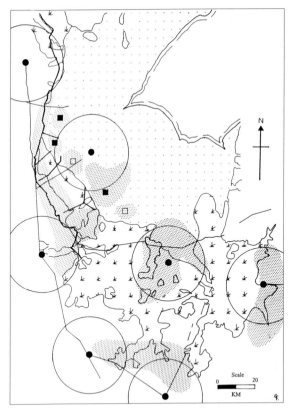

73 A map of the Fenland showing the Fenland communities, with the catchment areas of all of the probable markets identified in the region superimposed upon them. Markets in pre-industrial societies had catchment areas 5km in radius – the distance a farmer could walk there and back in a day. Note how most of the areas of settlement fall within range of a market

74 A map of community four (the general location of which is shown on 59)

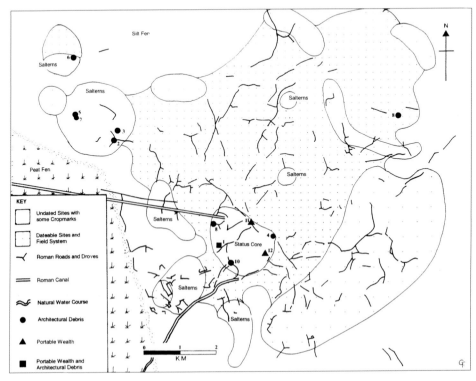

KEY

☐	Undated Sites with some Cropmarks
⬚	Dateable Sites and Field System
⌄	Roman Roads and Droves
═	Roman Canal
≋	Natural Water Course
●	Architectural Debris
▲	Portable Wealth
■	Portable Wealth and Architectural Debris

is unlikely that our traveller would be free simply to wonder east into the Fens. Perhaps permission would only be granted at special market times, or upon payment of a 'tax' upon the goods being taken to trade.

Passing the bailiff's complex, our trader begins his eastern journey along a road very similar to the Fen Causeway to the south, passing out on a raised causeway across the marsh, through thick banks of reeds. Far to the east, smoke and steam are to be seen hanging in the air – the salters are at work boiling brine. Eventually, as he moves slowly along this road, the reeds clear. Either side of the causeway are long, regular trenches, now filled with water. These are peat cuttings, places where peat has been cut away in blocks and carried away to be stacked and dried, ultimately to be used as fuel to fire the salterns.

He walks for over an hour through this quiet and largely empty land of reeds, peat and wild fowl. Our traveller finds himself at the edge of a community, and to either side of the road are groups of flat-bottomed, terracotta-coloured pans, standing in depressions in the ground. There is fire beneath them, Fenlanders are tending the flames, and the contents of the pans, brine, is boiling away to leave behind valuable salt. Amongst the salterns are small shacks made of roughly cut wood, the walls built up out of grey silty mud and roofed in reed thatch. These are the 'summer quarters', the crude huts that the salters occupy for a few months as they tend their boiling pits. The air here is thick with the mixture of peaty smoke and steam that the traveller could see from afar, and he hurries past, avoiding the sullen and hostile stares that the workers here reserve for outsiders.

This is not a pleasant place, and our traveller doesn't linger. He continues down the principal drove way, a green, grassy road with ditches and tightly laid hedge at either side to prevent the escape of livestock when they are driven to be slaughtered. He walks on until pasture fields and small, rough, daub-walled, thatched farmhouses replace the salterns and the peat cuttings. Here there are cattle and occasional storehouses where carcases are hung. They are waiting for the salt from the salterns, and then meat will be cured. There are also hides, stretched out on frames, drying in the sun – leather is a precious commodity, and certainly not to be wasted.

The traveller suddenly comes upon a different type of building. The walls are smooth and plastered, the roof an even one of tile. The traveller tenses slightly as he catches sight of it, sitting as it does on the edge of an open space in the centre of the community. There are others, all gathered in this central area – estate offices, official store rooms, and this is where the traveller is likely to run into figures of authority – people he is normally keen to avoid. Meekly he knocks on a door, and registers with the official there – he is here to sell at the little market where all the people hereabouts get their goods... yes, he'll set up straightaway, yes, he'll be gone by tomorrow. Where will he go? Back to the town.

Other traders are arriving, setting up small stalls in the green at the centre of the community: they are there to sell pottery, metal goods, nothing of particular value, just the basics of life that the Fenlanders cannot make for themselves. Trade

75 A reconstruction of the landscape of Roman Fenland, crossing the Peat Fen towards a settlement in the Silts. Note the peat cuttings either side of the road, where peat has been gathered for fuel, and the smoke rising around the buildings in the distance, salterns being fired. *Illustration by Melanie Cameron*

76 A map of community five (the general location of which is shown on *59*)

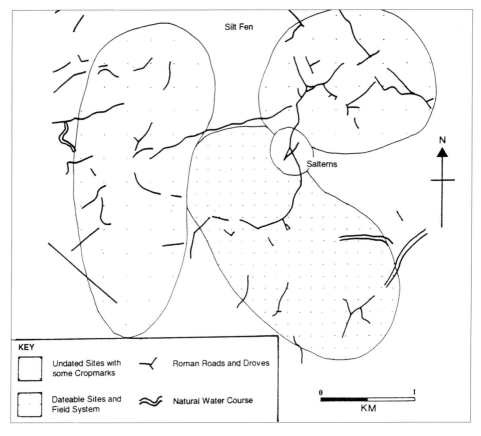

Silt Fen

Salterns

N

KEY

☐ Undated Sites with some Cropmarks

⊡ Dateable Sites and Field System

⌁ Roman Roads and Droves

≈ Natural Water Course

0 _____ 1

KM

77 The coastal fringes of the Fens, showing what untamed Silt Fen may have looked like

is slow – money is never plentiful out here on the Fens, and it is a particularly poor day's trading, with many of the farmers away at the salterns. The trader, however, cannot return to the town with some of his load of pottery unsold – unless he can sell it, he will not have the cash that he needs to buy produce from the Fenlanders, the produce that he is relying on taking back to Durobrivae. He decides that night to push on to the port, out by the coast.

Another journey down a Fenland road, heading further east, across a dark open landscape. At its end, he comes across a collection of wooden and stone buildings, clustered around a quayside. The port is small and often empty, but he is in luck. Two ships, cargo vessels of the Roman Fleet, are at anchor, loading up with salted meat and leather. When they sail, they will go north, delivering their cargo to the soldiers stationed far up the coast. Timidly, afraid of rebuke and punishment, the trader approaches the officer in charge of the loading, holding out a sample of his stock. The soldier pauses, looking at the pottery, then at the trader. The soldier holds up his hand and rubs his thumb and forefinger together – the soldier and the trader are from different parts of the empire, they do not know each other's language, but the meaning is clear, the language universal. The soldier wants a bribe – for the price of a few coins he will buy the stock from the trader, and take them north. There are always people on the emperor's wall that need pottery, and they will pay good money.

5

THE NENE VALLEY: KILNS, IRON AND VILLAS

An unusual characteristic of the town of Durobrivae, and one of the reasons why the town was chosen for this study, is the fact that it functions as the heart of a complex of industries, remarkable for Roman Britain. These are principally the iron-ore production sites of the East Midlands, sites like Whitwell and Empingham (where large amounts of iron-rich stone were processed during the Roman period) and the Nene Valley pottery industries. There was also a mosaic school which seems to have developed in the town in the very later period, but this is discussed in the next chapter. As we shall see, the development of these industries is intimately linked with the rise of the large villas which lie immediately to the west of the town, and spread some way up the valley.

We must begin by considering what we know about the pottery industry in this region. Pottery assemblages on sites that have been occupied during the Roman period are dominated at the start of the occupation by what we may term regional imports – that is pottery made in Britain, but not local, and imports from the empire beyond. Such classes of pottery are divided into two: coarse wares, a cheap form of pottery that may have been used every day, and fine wares that occur in much lesser quantities and which were probably used on more 'special' occasions. The arrival of the army in AD 47, and the construction of the forts at Longthorpe, at the crossing of the Nene, would have generated increased demand for 'Roman-style' pottery, firstly focusing upon the fort and the soldiers based there, but later on Roman-British sites as well. It is possible that itinerant potters, following the wake of the army and intent upon taking advantage of the ready market for their product provided by the military, were the first to introduce this kind of pottery to the area. The excavations at Longthorpe provide a clear starting point for regional pottery production – a large works depot was constructed to supply the fortress, and one of its principal products was pottery. This centre of production may have attracted native potters from other parts of the region, principally, perhaps, the middle and upper Nene, as well as some from further afield,

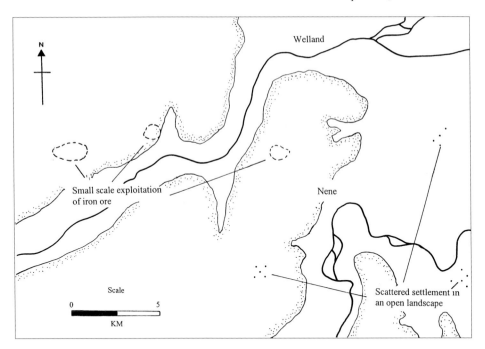

78 A generalised map of the western portion of Durobrivae's hinterland in the late Iron Age

like, for example, from the Rhine, where large numbers of potters were already working for the army. The departure of the soldiers from their base at the Nene Crossing, and indeed from the wider region at some point in the late first century, may have seen these itinerant potters moving on. However, by this point either local demand for the product had been established, or local potters had adopted the techniques of the army potters, and by AD 125-150 there were the beginnings of a local industry developing in the lower Nene Valley producing a range of products *(79* and *80)*. Nene Valley ware, associated with Samian of the second quarter of the second century AD, has been recovered from sites like Orton Hall Farm, the Normangate Field site (the northern suburb of Durobrivae) and Monument 97 (an early site, just to the west of Orton Hall Farm).

The Nene was the perfect location for a large-scale pottery industry which had begun to develop on the area, with all the essential ingredients nearby. There was water, clay and a surrounding forest to provide fuel to fire the kilns. It is likely that this forest lay principally to the north, a possibility tentatively identified by Mackreth on the basis that there is a limited amount of settlement in that area. Maybe more important (as there are many locations which never developed a pottery industry, where fuel, water and clay were available within a reasonable distance) were two other factors. Firstly, there were good transport links (north and south up Ermine Street, and east and west along the Nene), which allowed the products of the industry to be transported out of the area of production, and secondly, a ready market into which to sell the pots existed in the form of the

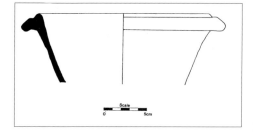

79 Grey ware bowl of the Nene Valley pottery industry. *Illustration by Gillian Hawkes*

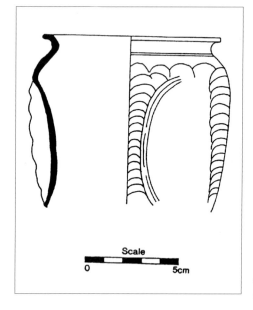

80 A scaled beaker, a colour-coated product of the Nene Valley pottery industry. *Illustration by Gillian Hawkes*

nearby town and it's dependent territories. The distribution of the kilns themselves is very clearly focused upon Durobrivae, occurring in some numbers to the north of the town, and spreading up the banks of the Nene to the west *(83)*. Some kilns have also been discovered to the east of the town, at Stanground (also on the Nene), and possibly to the south at Stilton. However, the distribution area of Nene Valley products from these kilns goes well beyond this local market, which sees Nene Valley ware come to dominate the Fens and the Nene Valley itself – and examples of this pottery occur as far north as Hadrian's Wall. The widespread occurrence of this pottery is something to which we will return later, because it is something which will help us to understand why this industry, and others in the region, grew as they did.

What do we know about of the technology of the Nene Valley industry? First, we must examine the basic structure of a Romano-British kiln, the central piece of technology required to produce ceramics *(82)*. Although there are variations, the basic principle that lies behind different types of Roman-British kiln is the same. The pots to be fired are enclosed in the body of kiln. At the bottom of the kiln will be a flue or fire tunnel. It might be that the pots are rested on the ground surface, or on the floor of a pit dug into the ground, and that the fire is built in the flue. An exhaust vent at the top of the body of the kiln encourages hot air from the fire to circulate between the pots and eventually out through the vent. In more sophisticated kilns, the pots will be rested upon a 'floor', supported by piers and columns. The flue will lead into the 'under-floor' space, and it is here (beneath the floor) that the fire will be located, allowing a greater and more even circulation of heat *(84)*. There are no Nene Valley pottery kilns dating to before the late second/early third centuries, so those associated with the Nene Valley industry, being relatively late, are of the more sophisticated variety. One, excavated in Normangate Field by the antiquarian Artis and carefully illustrated and published in a book of plates in 1828, had a circular body which had been lined with pre-fired curved clay blocks, especially built for the purpose, and appears, from the illustration, to be one of the most sophisticated kilns discovered in the area, and indeed in the whole province. The lining will have helped retain heat within the body of the kiln, thus allowing the pots to be fired at a higher temperature *(84 and 85)*.

The products of the industry fall into two principal categories. The first is grey ware, a utilitarian, minimally decorated range of items, principally dishes, flagons and jars, probably used for cooking and everyday use. The second type of pottery produced was Nene Valley colour-coated ware. Pots were dipped in a slip and then fired, giving them a dark sheen. This sheen was applied to a variety of forms,

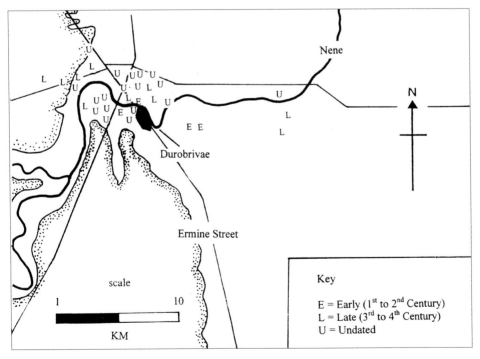

81 Map of the kiln sites of the Nene Valley pottery industry, showing how the kilns cluster in the vicinity of the town

82 Left The excavation of a typical Roman-British kiln. Although this example is from Sussex, the main features of all Romano-British pottery kilns (including those of the Nene Valley) are visible. The stoke hole is at the top of the picture, pottery and fragments of the kiln floor are also visible. Note the earth piers at the left of the picture which would have supported the floor

83 Right Kiln furniture from a Nene Valley kiln excavated at Stibbington. A fire bar can be seen at the top of the picture, with fragments of kiln floor below (see *84* and *85*). Note the fifty pence piece for scale

including beakers, flagons, jars and the so-called 'castor box' form (large high-sided dishes with a lid). Perhaps the most famous of these vessels, the so-called 'hunt cups' were small beakers, probably used for drinking, and were decorated with what is termed 'barbotine', the decoration being applied to the body of the pot and the patterns squeezed onto the vessel rather in the manner of cake icing. The vessels carry shapes, or scenes involving animals, some of which appear to be being hunted by human figures, hence the name 'hunt cup'.

If the industry had its beginnings in AD 125–150, how did it develop in the centuries that followed? By AD 175–200 both elements of production, the colour-coat, and the grey ware, were firmly established. The 'repertoire' (the range of shapes produced by an industry) of grey wares remained fairly standard, simple, utilitarian forms until a decline in production in the fourth century. This utilitarian pottery is less intensively studied than colour-coat, so this apparent uniformity and stability in grey ware production may be at least partly due to ignorance on our part about the way the industry developed. However, we do know much more about colour coat production. Beakers were a popular element of this, perhaps being particularly so in the third century (AD 200–300), although the

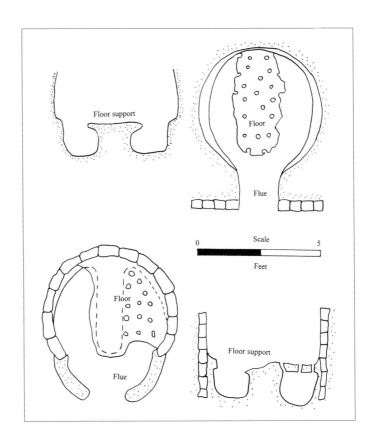

84 Plans of two
excavated kilns from
Stibbington. *After
Hartley, 1960*

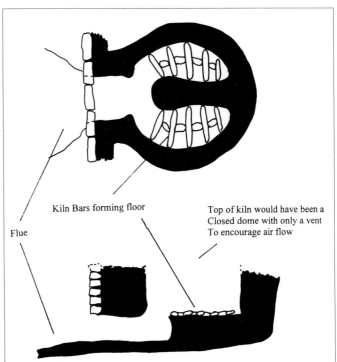

85 Schematic diagram
of the structure of a
Nene Valley kiln. The
floor in this kiln is made
up of bars supported by
a single, central pier.
After Swann, 1984

detail of their design changed over time. Another popular form, the 'castor box', was produced with minor variations from the start of the industry into the fourth century, possibly right to the end of Nene Valley ware production in the first half of the fifth (AD 400–450). Fourth-century production also included forms previously produced as grey ware, like flagons and some dishes.

A final key element of late fourth-century production was imitation Samian ware. Samian was an important type of Roman pottery, hard, red, and common on many sites from the Conquest onwards. It was produced in Gaul, and remained an important source of fine ware in Britain until the decline of the industry in the third century. Demand for such wares continued in Britain, however, and imitations of Samian dishes, platters, jars, bowls and jugs were all made by the Nene Valley potters in this late period.

The industry as a whole came to an end in the fifth century, with the end of the Roman occupation. The exact timing of the end of production is problematic, and as with many other issues surrounding the fifth century there is simply very little evidence upon which to base a judgement. However, a sherd (a fragment of a broken pot) found at Orton Hall Farm may give us a clue. The fragment was from a mortarium, a Roman form, but in a Saxon fabric (the material that the pottery is made from), and thus seems to belong to the second quarter of the fifth century (AD 425–450). This is a small piece of evidence, but does seem to suggest that production of Roman-style pottery continued for at least a while after the occupation. To suggest that the industry declined in the first quarter of the fifth century, and finally ceased production in AD 425–450 is perhaps little more than an educated guess, but given our limited information this is probably the best picture of the end of Nene Valley ware that we can reach.

The history of the industry is not the only aspect that we need to consider. As noted above, Nene Valley ware was available over a wide area. In fact, it has been found not only in the area of production, the Nene Valley and Durobrivae, but also across the Fens, down into the Thames Valley and into Kent. It occurs on sites across the heart of England, and as far west as the coast of south Wales. It is found occasionally in the south-west, and on scattered sites across the north of England. It is also found all along Hadrian's Wall, with some also being found on the Antonine Wall, its later and more northern counterpart, that runs through southern Scotland. Nene Valley ware has even been recovered from the wreck of a small cargo ship which sank in Guernsey harbour between AD 275 and 325, and was probably in the process of being exported to the continent. To explain this distribution area we must understand how that industry was organised, and the factors which generated a local willingness to create and maintain an industry on such a scale. To do this, we need to look back at the beginning of the Roman occupation in this area, to a period when there was an unusually intense military presence in the region.

We have already discussed the fortress at Longthorpe, possibly housing up to half a legion, and there was also the small fort, guarding the crossing of the river

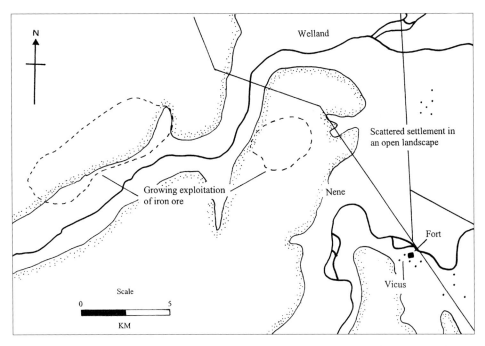

86 Generalised map of the western portion of Durobrivae's hinterland in the first century, after the Roman conquest

itself – of great strategic importance *(86)*. In addition, there are the military installations in the Fens, at, for example, Grandford, which was probably a satellite outpost of Longthorpe. However there then appears in the archaeology to be a break of some forty years between the abandonment of these military establishments and the rise of the town of Durobrivae, which, in the form that it is familiar to us, was principally an Antonine creation of the second century. We must be conscious of the fact that the lack of archaeological investigation in the town means that our understanding of its development is imperfect, but if the crossing were important to the Romans in the Conquest period, it also remained so later. It was significant enough in the second century to encourage successful settlement – the location of Durobrivae probably being influenced by the crossing. Why, then, for the fifty years between the two occupations, are we suggesting that the crossing seemed to have no importance at all to the authorities? It seems much more likely that we simply are not aware, yet, of the Roman involvement in the area during these 'missing' forty years.

If it seems likely that there was continuity between the period of the forts and the town, perhaps in the form of a small settlement beneath the later development of Durobrivae that is obscured by the Antonine settlement, what might the significance of this be? The answer to this is tied up with the salt production on the Fens. It has been suggested that this production, although not directly run as an operation by the Roman authorities, was tendered out to local elites. We might

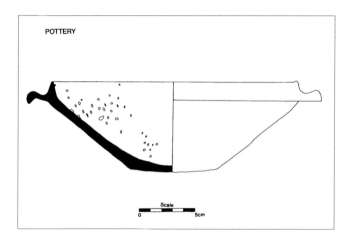

POTTERY

Scale
0   5cm

87 Mortarium (mixing bowl), a product of the Nene Valley industry. *Illustration by Gillian Hawkes*

suggest that this was intimately linked with the early Roman military presence in the area – the one authority in Roman Britain which required large amounts of raw material and food, and had the manpower and authority to acquire it, was the Roman army. It seems likely that, the forts being located in this area, the army became aware of the local salt industry. It may also have been the army's responsibility to run the imperial monopoly of this commodity (it has been suggested above that the authorities would have awarded contracts to locals to actually produce the salt), and organise the local industry to ensure that the imperial authorities had ultimate control of it. Part of this role may have also been to increase production to ensure that sufficient salt for the supply of the army was delivered. Having tapped into a local resource and spent effort in increasing production, it seems unlikely that, when the army moved on, they would just abandon a good source of salt, and we might envisage leaving a small military presence as suggested in Chapter Two. This may have consisted of no more than a centurion and a few supporting men.

We have already recounted how, in the early years of the occupation, following the Boudican revolt, the area appears to have been reorganised (like, for example, the suggested removal of the Central Fens from the jurisdiction of the Iceni, and the re-allocation of this area, and its salt production, to the Corieltauvi). But here, we may remind ourselves that this had the twin effect of not only punishing a tribe that had rebelled (removing a source of tribal wealth), but also of centralising Iron Age salt production in the region into the hands of one tribe, the Corieltauvi. As the settlements on the east coast of the Fens, the former beneficiaries of Central Fen salt wealth, declined, settlements, especially that of Durobrivae on the west developed. The reorganised salt production industry would have helped to stimulate the growth of the town. With the army interested in the region, the local elites grew rich upon the benefits of empire – seizing the opportunity the army and the salt had offered them. The continuing link which allowed them to seize such opportunities may have been the small

88 Right Sherds from a
mortarium. Note the grit on the
inside of the vessel, allowing
the grinding of food. *Photograph
by Gillian Hawkes*

89 Below Generalised map of
the western portion of
Durobrivae's hinterland in the
second century

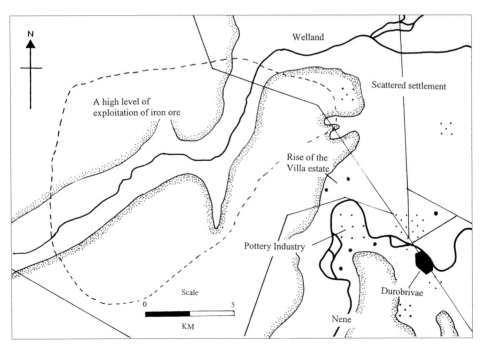

N

Welland

Scattered settlement

A high level of
exploitation of iron ore

Rise of the
Villa estate

Pottery Industry

Durobrivae

Scale

0   5

KM

Nene

military staff envisaged above, particularly if it were charged with organising and dispensing supply contracts for the army proper which had now moved on. The logical place for such a staff to be based would, of course, be the early pre-Antonine beginnings of Durobrivae.

How does this relate to pottery? The pottery industry of the region grew long after this period of transition between direct military control and the rise of the town *(89)*. The relationship formed between the army and this area is, however, fundamental to explaining the remarkable growth of this industry, even if it occurs in a later period. Pottery is both heavy and fragile, and cannot be traded long distances without great expense because of its bulk and fragility. This must cause us to ask how Nene Valley ware came to be being traded up to Hadrian's Wall? Without some factor which transcends pure market economics (which would dictate that the Wall be supplied with pottery from kilns as close as possible to where military units were, thus minimising transport costs), such a situation could never have arisen. The phenomenon of the relative popularity of Nene Valley ware on the Wall clearly illustrates that some military link to the area of pottery production existed, even long after the army had moved on from forts like Longthorpe. But how did this link work? The army was the one institution in Roman Britain which supplied itself upon such a large scale that pottery might easily be made hundreds of miles away from where it was produced, but this does not, in itself, explain why the pottery came from the Durobrivae area. The primary trade between this area and the army was probably in salt (as well as salt meat, and by-products of meat like leather and wool) and iron. The military occupation of the Nene Crossing area, made necessary by the strategic nature of that crossing, was sufficient to form the initial link. The army in essence became aware of the resources being produced in the area, albeit on a small scale. The need for the army to secure supplies will have been enough to stimulate activity of a greater scale in both of these industries (possibly resulting from the direct intervention of military officials to boost production levels). Such supply sources continued to supply the army after the military units had moved on, the army being prepared to ship commodities great distances from supply sources that they knew. With this trade established, the shipping of pottery, perhaps a few pots at a time, on ships laden with meat, and other goods destined for the army, becomes easier to understand. The principal connection with the army was that the area around Durobrivae, the Fens to the east and the uplands to west, remained a significant region for military supply, even as the army moved north. But a by-product of what must have been a major logistic effort was the ability to piggy-back other products (i.e. pottery) on these key commodities, and send them north. Transport costs were effectively subsidised by the principal trade in salt and iron, and their related products. It should be noted of course, that trade was largely in commodities that are perishable, and so hard to detect archaeologically, as they leave no archaeological trace. But we can discern that greater trade, because the lesser one in pottery did leave us a trace in the archaeological record – that of shattered and discarded Nene

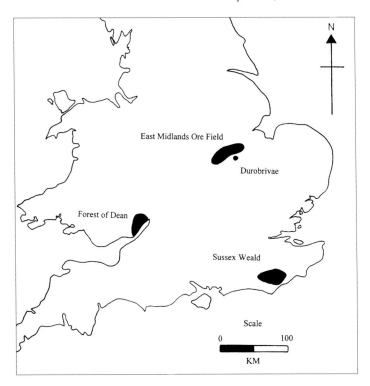

90 A map showing the different areas of iron working in the province of Britain

Valley colour-coat discarded on the Wall. The rise of the pottery industry, then, was closely connected to the military contracts for other products, but also relied upon an entrepreneurial class of people, presumably those already running the salt trade for the Roman authorities, to take advantage of another opportunity that empire had offered them.

We can see similar forces at work in the development of the mining of iron ore. A history of the iron-mining and smelting industry in the East Midlands is difficult to establish, as research into this field is only in its infancy. However, we can sketch the main developments of production for the late Iron Age and the Roman periods. Before the Conquest there was iron-mining activity, but on a small scale, fulfilling perhaps a purely local demand, and focused on the iron-bearing deposits of the Jurassic ridge in Northamptonshire, just to the west of where Durobrivae would grow up in the second century. In this Iron Age phase of activity smelting (the process of turning iron ore into pure iron) probably took place close to where the ore was mined in order to minimise transport costs. But demand for iron increased sharply with the arrival of the Roman army in the East Midlands in about AD 47. For the army iron would have been a key resource, used for everything from nails to armour and, as with salt, the military were clearly attracted to any existing sources of iron ore. The two areas traditionally considered the principal sources of iron in Roman Britain, the Sussex Weald and the Forest of Dean, were both associated with military exploitation at some stage of their

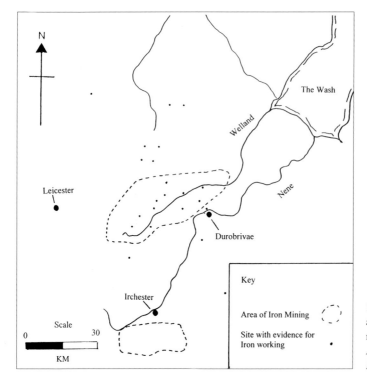

91 Map showing the area of ore mining in relation to the town. *After Jones and Mattingly, 1990*

history, the former by the Roman fleet, the *Classis Britannica*, and the latter by the legionary forts at Cardiff and Caerwent, as well as the fort at Gloucester *(90)*. In the case of the East Midlands we have a clear and early link between the military and local iron working. The Longthorpe Fortress and its attached depot seem to have been the sight of smelting activity, suggesting that in the early years after the Conquest, supplies of ore were diverted to the military for their own use.

Increasing demand throughout the Roman period led to a steady increase in the number of production sites, focused upon regional communication ways (roads and rivers). This clearly indicates that the products of the industry were intended for a wider than purely local market; they were intended to be 'shipped out' to other areas. Commentators have drawn analogies between the iron industry, salt production in the Fens, and the production of Nene Valley ware pottery, which were all major industries with wide distributions. This might suggest that the East Midlands iron production industry may have ranked along side the two traditionally pre-eminent centres mentioned earlier, the Forest of Dean and the Sussex Weald, as a source of iron that was of provincial significance. The industry appears to have declined sharply with the end of the Roman period, possibly for reasons similar to those already outlined for other Roman period industries. However, the natural resources of the area continued to attract attention, and the medieval period saw a regrowth in iron production, an activity which continued into modern times.

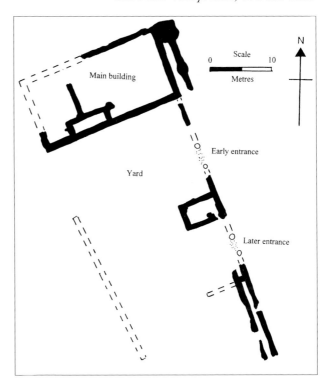

92 Empingham, a site in the East Midlands that was involved in the small-scale smithing of iron. *After Cooper, 2000*

As the importance of the industry grew, its products would need to be funnelled through market towns, and the iron-producing area of the East Midlands may well have been served by some or all of the market towns surrounding it. These include Leicester (Ratae Corieltavorum), the *colonia* at Lincoln (Lindum), and, of course, Durobrivae. However, the geographical distribution of the ore-production and smelting sites, resting in an arc running around Durobrivae, approximately from the west of the town to the north, clearly makes Durobrivae the natural centre of this industry *(91)*. We also have more direct evidence linking the two. Not only do we have the early connection between the iron industry and Durobrivae area through the smelting attested at the Longthorpe Fortress, but we have direct evidence of such metal-working activity from the town itself, located in the Normangate suburb.

We thus have a broad outline of the industry, but can we say anything about the way that it was actually organised? Ore was, by and large, smelted close to the site where it was mined, thus ensuring that only pure metal was transported to reduce costs. This means, however, that large amounts of waste produced by the smelting process were left behind. This process took place largely in scattered rural settlements, but recent research indicates that such settlements were producing smelted iron at different levels of intensity. A site smelting iron might be working on a small scale, based on household activity – an individual may be engaged in a little working with iron, smithing, or repairing iron items, perhaps to supplement

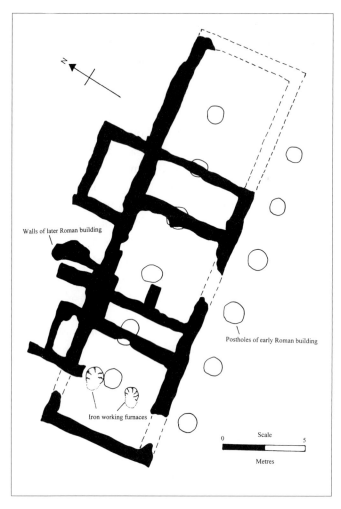

Walls of later Roman building

Postholes of early Roman building

Iron working furnaces

Scale

0   5

Metres

93 Left Plan of the central villa building at Whitwell. Note the iron-smelting furnaces on the same site. *After Todd, 1981*

94 Below Detail of the furnaces from Whitwell. *After Todd, 1981*

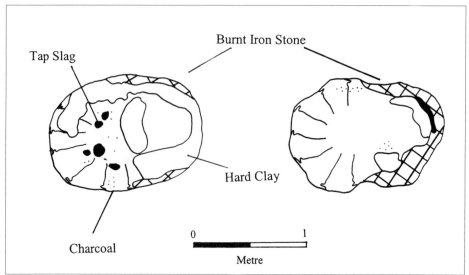

Tap Slag

Burnt Iron Stone

Hard Clay

Charcoal

0   1

Metre

a broadly agricultural lifestyle, like at Empingham *(92)*. The next step up might be a small settlement with several furnaces working at the same time, though this might still be primarily as a supplement to other activities, like in Whitwell. In this case, but particularly with the small-scale 'household' activity of the first level of production, it is possible that iron working, as with salt and pottery production, might have been a seasonal activity, with the economy of particular sites being dependent upon a range of different activities which could be conducted at different times of the year. The final level of intensity was a fully 'industrialised' site, in which there were many furnaces, and in which iron production was the principal activity. What we find in the East Midlands is that the industry functioned with a mixture of these different types of sites simultaneously. Particularly interesting are the villa sites of Whitwell *(93)* and Piddington, where small numbers of furnaces have been identified, and which might be typical of low intensity production, conducted on a 'household' or individual 'estate' basis, and for a considerable period of time. Evidence from Whitwell, for example, suggests that iron production was taking place on this site in from the middle of the first century AD, maybe until as late as the late fourth century *(94)*. The importance of the Whitwell and Piddington examples are that they demonstrate a link between the exploitation of iron ore and the local villa-owning class, something which we will pick up upon later.

Examination of the technology used in the iron-production/working industry shows a similarly varied and somewhat piecemeal character to that seen in its organisation. The 'domed' furnace, in use in the pre-Roman industry of the area, remained in use, quite possibly right through the Roman period. These were used alongside more sophisticated shaft furnaces (of both the tall and short shafted varieties), which probably began use in the early second century. There are also

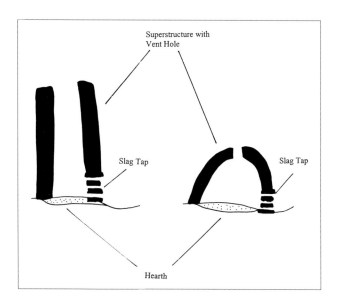

95 Shaft and dome iron furnaces. Both types were used in the East Midlands. *After McWhirr, 1982*

examples of the advanced 'bowl' furnace type *(95)*. This variation in the type of technology in use argues against any centrally directed drive at making more iron, in which we might expect to see large numbers of the same type of furnace, constructed and run by the authorities. Rather, what we are seeing are individual choices upon what type of furnace to construct, a decision based perhaps upon a variety of factors, like knowledge (what type of furnace the individual concerned knew how to build), or how much iron the furnace was expected to smelt.

The existence of different levels of production and the simultaneous use of different types of furnace suggests a rather *ad hoc* growth in the industry, which developed at a slower rate to the iron industries in, for example, the Forest of Dean and Sussex, which might be related to the way in which the various industries of the Durobrivae area were interconnected, and the way in which production in the region as a whole was organised. It is probable that the Roman authorities were closely involved in the mining and refining of iron ore in the East Midlands. Like salt, leather, wool and pottery, iron was a crucial requirement of the Roman army, and used by them for everything from swords and armour to nails. The expansion of the industry is likely to have been motivated, or at least enabled at some level, by the military requirements for processed raw materials and finished objects. However, any suggested relationship between iron production and the military needs to explain why the industry appears, as noted, to have developed in such an 'organic', piecemeal fashion. There are two principal scenarios through which this may have come about.

In the first scenario, if, as argued in Chapters Three and Four, salt production had been specifically encouraged by the authorities, and pottery production grew up on the back of that, iron from the Nene Valley area would also have made its way into the system of army supply. Perhaps, like the salt, iron production was specifically encouraged by the authorities for their own requirements. The *ad hoc* nature of the industry argues against a high degree of intervention, but perhaps pressure on the local elites to produce what was required led to an intensification of production. This would have led to intensification that took place through a range of individual decisions, rather than in any centrally planned fashion controlled directly by the military. This, then, might have led to increased production, but taking place through a variety of different technological technique, and at different levels of intensity on different settlements.

The alternative is the same as the scenario presented for the development of the pottery industry, not so much one of coercion of the elite, but engagement by them with the Roman authorities. A local resource, in this case iron ore, was required by the Roman army. Being aware of this need, the local elites took it upon themselves to supply the army with what they wanted, and in so doing realised that the more they could produce, the more they would be able to sell. This would have led to an intensification of production, and in an *ad hoc* way – but the impetus would have come from the elite, using the region's links with the army to their advantage. In either scenario, the production of iron ore in the

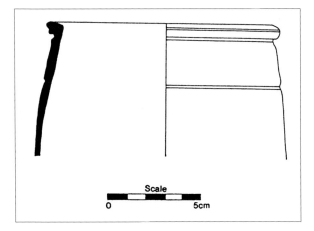

96 A beaker. A product of the Nene Valley industry, traded with the Roman Army in the north, and common on Hadrian's Wall. *Illustration by Gillian Hawkes*

region seems to be no coincidence: Durobrivae was a major centre for supplying the Roman army with its requirements, and we may strongly suggest that this close link with the army was the basis of Durobrivae's industrial success, and that the scale of industry around Durobrivae was supported not by any form of successful market economy, but by the economically artificial stimulus of a number of army supply 'contracts'.

As mentioned above, the East Midlands' ore fields were one of three possible major production centres for iron in the province, the other two being the Sussex Weald and the Forest of Dean. There is only sketchy evidence of how and why the East Midlands production area developed and was run, but we can learn a little more about it by comparison with these other two areas. In the Forest of Dean we see a small Iron Age production industry which, like the East Midlands, attracted the attention of the military in the period immediately following the Conquest, with a consequent increase in demand. In the Forest of Dean production grew rapidly in the first century AD, and into the second, with levels of production plateauing in the third century and declining in the late Roman period. As with the East Midlands, the focus of production was settlement sites, rather than specialist industrial sites, and as with the East Midlands there were differing scales of production, perhaps suggesting 'independent' production in both areas. However, unlike the East Midlands, the ore seems to have been transported some distance before being smelted, and the major smelting site, Ariconium, lay outside the forest, beyond the principal mining area.

The Sussex Weald also saw the development of iron working with a military association, perhaps focused upon the port of Bodium *(98)*. Here also, as with the East Midlands and the Forest of Dean, there is evidence for pre-Roman production on a small scale. The Roman industry was sizeable, with two main groups of sites, one on the coast in the Hastings area, and one further inland on the Wealden plain. The coastal group seems to have developed first, being largely active by the end of the first century, and some sites in the inland group were also

97 Typical rolling scenery of the iron-producing area of Durobrivae's hinterland

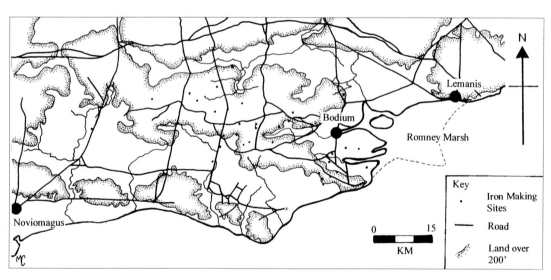

98 A map showing the Sussex Weald, and the distribution of iron-working sites. Note how the sites cluster around the trading centre of Bodium. *Illustration by Melanie Cameron*

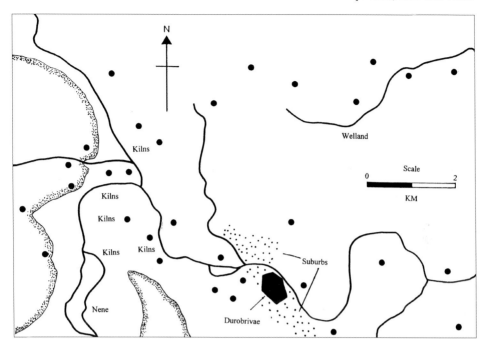

99 Durobrivae and the villas of the Nene Valley

active by this period. A second general phase of activity saw greater exploitation of the inland reserves. By the late third century the industry was in decline, maybe because of over-exploitation, with many of the small iron-ore deposits worked out and possible deforestation leading to lack of fuel. However, the rise of production elsewhere, like in the Forest of Dean, may also have seen demand for the Sussex metal decrease. Military involvement in the running of this industry is perhaps more clear-cut than in other cases: clay tiles stamped with an inscription linking them to the *Classis Britannica*, the Roman fleet stationed in the channel, have been found on many iron-working sites in Sussex (like that, for example, of Beauport Park, Battle).

By looking at three major iron-producing areas we see a general pattern of a pre-Roman industry, expanding in scale under military encouragement, and focused through one or more urban centres. This is, as we have seen, also a model that seems to apply to some of the other industries of the Durobrivae hinterland, that is salt and pottery production. What we have so far not addressed is how the different industries were interrelated with each other, and the wider social structure of the area, as well as how the link with the military may have worked in practice. To explain this, we must look at the relationship between these industries and the villas of the Nene Valley.

The villas of the lower Nene Valley are well known. They are strung out along the Nene, separated by an average distance of between ten and twenty miles, and

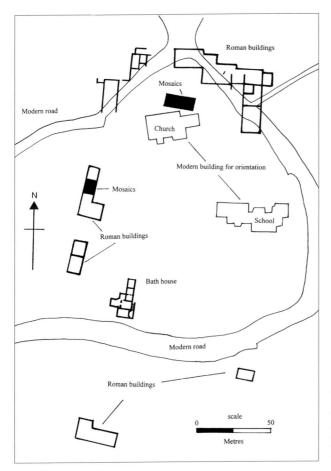

100 Plan of the large villa beneath the village of Castor, and partially excavated by Artis. See *9* for one of Artis' plates illustrating the excavation

cluster in the immediate vicinity of Durobrivae with at least three close to the western edge of the town. How these houses developed is, like the town itself, a little vague, due to a lack of modern excavation, but the elaborate buildings that we know of are probably the late Roman phases of establishments with a longer history. What is certain is that the landscape to the west of the town was intensively farmed, and it has been suggested by Wild, given the limited number of late villa estates, that a process of aggregation took place. This would mean that smaller farms in the early Roman period were absorbed by progressively larger estates as time passed, a process which perhaps began as early as the second century *(99)*.

The late Roman period in this area was one, if the villas are anything to go by, of great prosperity, the establishments that survived until the fourth century showing evidence for increasing wealth. A prime example is the 'palatial' structure under the village of Castor, so large that it has variously be considered to be the 'headquarters' of the Fenland estates of the emperor, or even the residence of the 'Duke of the Saxon Shore', a late Roman military official in charge of the defences of Britain *(100)*. Others interpret this as simply the house of a very wealthy landowner, and other villas, like Great Weldon, also show expansion and wealth at this period – a mosaic floor dating to the late half of the fourth century (AD 350–400) was found here. It is thus clear that the villa estates generally entered a period of some prosperity, and there is evidence of wider economic vitality, with a local mosaics 'school' (a group of craftsmen working together and developing a common style in the production of mosaic pavements) well established. The continued strength of the Nene Valley potteries, which were in production throughout the fourth century, also points in this direction.

How do the villas relate to the industries which we discussed earlier? The key to the relationship between the different elements of the landscape is the crucial issue of land ownership. We have already noted the fact that land was probably owned and sold in small parcels. The pattern of small parcels of land is one that we note across the empire. A prime example comes from Pliny's discussion of his villa at Laurentine about which he writes at length in Book Two of his collected letters to his friend Gallus, and how it forms part of his 'estate', meaning a variety of landholdings in different places. We also see it in documents recovered from Egypt, specifically from the papers of the Appianus estate, an archive which preserves a picture of the day-to-day working of Roman agriculture. Here it is noted that in a particular village several of the big estates of the area own property, and have offices in the village to manage their affairs, a situation similar to that we have outlined for the Silt Fen communities. The first point to be drawn from this is that landholding, not just in the Fens, but also in Durobrivae and the Nene Valley, was probably very fragmented. We cannot think of estates as large

101 Pottery was produced to the west of Durobrivae

continuous areas of land, with a villa neatly at its heart – Roman estates, rather like modern large farms and estates, would have consisted of holdings spread across the landscape. The estates that grew up around Durobrivae, then, in the second and third century, would have consisted of various different elements which reflected the diverse financial interests of the landholder. Such a typical estate would consist, perhaps, of groups of salterns scattered through the different Silt Fen communities, with an office to administer them in a tiled building at the heart of the drove-way system. The estate, if it owned many of the salterns, might even employ a bailiff, living at one of the Fen Edge settlements that gave access to the Fens, to ensure some control over what was being taken in and out of the salt-production area. In addition such an estate might have an interest in the pottery industry, owning a section of the riverbank and the valley bottom where kilns were constructed to produce pottery for sale in the town market, or for export further afield. The iron-working industry might have functioned in a similar way. We have already noted that smelting has been discovered on actual villa sites like Whitwell and Piddington. Individual estate owners may well have operated small iron-ore mining operations within the East Midlands iron-production area, contributing to the profits of their wider estate interests.

If the villas which developed in the Nene Valley were at the heart of estates with interests across the hinterland, can we say anything about how they related to the town itself? Durobrivae would have performed two principal functions for the region which it controlled, a political/legal function and an economic one. The economic one we have already discussed in part, to organise the local industries and to provide a market centre for them. But the other function, the political/legal, we have not yet examined. The town council, the *Ordo*, would have had the function of administering the area. The *Ordo* would have been made up of perhaps 100 members called *decurions*, men of local wealth and standing – in the context of Durobrivae men drawn from the villa-owning class. The council itself elected two pairs of leading magistrates on an annual basis, essentially the 'executive officers' of the town's governing bodies. These officials were termed the *duoviri iuridicundo* (the more senior) and the *aediles*. Within the Roman world, however, power was granted, at a local level at least, in return for a *quid pro quo*: those that wielded such power accepted that in exchange they had to exercise some sense of responsibility. Those serving upon such councils were expected to spend their money for the good of the town – what we might call 'public munificence'. In pursuing such munificence a local official might be called upon to help fund the construction of a needed public building, or the restoration of an existing one that required repair. They might be called upon to contribute to the cost of city walls, or perhaps to pay for entertainments. Thus to serve upon such a council an individual had to be wealthy and, logically, in the area of Durobrivae and the surrounding territory. This means the villa/estate-owning classes. Such individuals would, however, have been able to exercise considerable influence over the town's market, perhaps controlling any taxation on what was sold. They may have influenced

102 A reconstruction of the potters' workshop excavated at Stibbington. *Illustration by Melanie Cameron*

what was brought into the town in the first place, which would have been significant for the people that controlled the industries and agriculture that was producing most of what was being sold. The elites may also have had a physical interest in the town, as well as political and economic. The many fine domestic structures that were constructed within the urban centre may well have been the 'town houses' of the rural rich, just one more property belonging to the 'portfolio' of the holdings of each estate. When we consider this picture of elite domination of the town alongside the landscape in the Fens, which we have already established as one of extreme control, we see that the villa-owning class were not only powerful, they may have come to dominate most aspects of local life to an extreme degree.

So, how do we envisage the estates around Durobrivae in the mid-Roman period working, and how does this help us to understand how the key aspects of the landscape may have functioned together? The best way to achieve this is to try to imagine a hypothetical estate. The estate would have been owned by a reasonably well-off local landowner who would have his main residence at one of the villas in the Nene Valley. This individual would have served his time on the town council and contributed his share towards the erection of public buildings there. If his villa was a fair distance from the town it might even be that he owned one of the large rich houses within the walls of the town. The estate of this landowner would have been highly fragmented – not a large extent of land around the main building, but individual holdings, scattered here and there across the landscape, perhaps separated by some distance. We might envisage an owner that had an estate which included some salt production, a little pottery production, and, of course, agricultural production. The villa itself might have been situated on the edge of the Nene Valley, a little west of the town. Below it, in the valley itself, a number of kilns may have operated along the riverbank, where they had access to water, clay and fuel from nearby woodland. The salt-working element of the estate might be in the form of a number of salterns round the edges of the Silt Fen communities, with a few accompanying fields in the more settled zones of the Fens. In each of the communities where this estate had property there might be an 'estate office' located in one of the tiled-roofed buildings at the core of the settled area.

The estate would thus be largely self-sufficient in pottery, salt and agricultural produce, with surpluses being traded through Durobrivae to provide the estate with an income. A system of periodic regional markets, *nundinae*, may well have been in operation, the landowner organising the sale of products made in one part of his estate (e.g. pottery), to those inhabiting another (e.g. in the Fens). This would have limited the amount of wealth that left the estate economy through the purchase of the products of a rival estate. The estate is unlikely to have been big enough to have been totally self-sufficient in all regards – note that our estate owner had no financial interest in the iron industry, and such goods may have been brought into the estate economy through trading at Durobrivae, or even by individual peddlers bringing goods from other estates, or other regions, onto the regular 'estate' markets.

If this gives us some idea of how the different parts of this landscape to the west of the town interrelated, what might such a landscape have seemed like to someone travelling through it? We have followed our travelling pot peddler from the south, up Ermine Street, and then east out into the Central and then the Silt Fens. He has bought his wares at a market in Durobrivae, and sold them amongst the salt workers to the east in the Fens. But now he is walking back towards the town, looking to acquire more goods to trade. He walks back south, down Ermine Street, back into the town of Durobrivae. The market here has closed and will not open again for several days, but he knows that this is still summer, still the kiln-firing season, and that, with luck, he will be able to buy new stock direct from the potters. With this in mind he turns for the road west.

This road runs through the town defences, and across the flood plain of the River Nene, following the valley into the upland, and out into the wider territory of the town. Leaving the walls and the expensive town houses behind, our traveller comes first across the great Nene Valley villas. These are strung out along the valley, mostly set a little back from the river on higher ground, giving better protection from flooding and, perhaps just as importantly for their inhabitants, better views. But along the waterfront is a different story. Lower in the valley, where there is a plentiful supply of water and clay, is where the kiln fields have been established. At its height, along this part of the river, there are large numbers of kilns, firing through the summer months. As with salt production, the firing of kilns requires good dry fuel to light them, and the woods a little to the north are regularly cut back, wood being bundled and hauled down to the valley for use as

103 A reconstruction of a section of the Nene Valley in the second or third century. A small villa looks down over firing pottery kilns. *Illustration by Melanie Cameron*

fuel. Wood doesn't burn so well when it's wet, so the kilns will have required a few days of reasonable weather to allow them to 'fire' their load of pottery. As with the salt workings to the east, this industry is not something that it is possible to pursue all year round. Farmers, in quiet periods in their work and when the sun is shining, turn to the kilns to make a little extra money, but these workers, like the inhabitants of the saltern communities and the Central Fens, are tenants of the local elites. Whilst it may be true that by engaging in pottery production these farmers are better off than they might have been, the real beneficiaries are the villa owners.

Although as he has walked along the road, through the kiln fields, he has tried to purchase a few pots off the potters, they are too wary to part with any of what they have produced – they were fired for the villa estate owners, and are not really the property of the kiln workers. But eventually, at a group of kilns well out of sight of the villas, the travelling pot seller manages to replenish his stock, a furtive deal done whilst no one is looking, a few coins changing hands, and baskets loaded with pottery, packed out with straw to prevent them breaking, hauled up and secured quickly to the back of the mule. He carries on along the road, roughly parallel to the river and running along the valley, rising ever higher. The landscape changes, becoming more open, and he leaves the cultivated areas of intense agriculture behind him. There is smoke rising in the distance – the thick black smoke of smelting iron ore. The road carries him over a heath, eventually into an area where the ground has been scraped bare, gravel and rock revealed. Large pits have been gouged in the surface, pits where the locals have recovered iron-rich rock. All around are furnaces, smoking domes where the ore is being refined, heated to release the molten metal. These people, like the salt workers and the pottery makers, are tenants of the great estates that focus upon the Nene Valley villas, and here they use nothing that has not been supplied to them by the estate of which they are a part. Out in this industrial area the estate owners contrive not only to extend their control by regulating what goods people can get access to, but also to ensure that any profit to be made is shared with the estate. The travelling peddler has already paid a fee to sell in the salt works of the east; he does so again to sell pottery to the iron smelters of the west.

6

THE LATE TOWN:
MOSAICS AND POTTERY

So far we have looked at the landscape around the town, and its development up to the end of the second century. This is the century during which the landscape became fully developed, and all of the various aspects which we see in the hinterland of the town are visible. It is the point at which Durobrivae and its hinterland are at their height. But it would be a mistake to consider the landscape of the town in static terms – reaching this point of development and then ceasing to evolve. Landscapes are continuously changing and are dynamic, and having reached a stage of being a mature and well-developed Roman town with established industries,and strong links with the now distant, but still supply-hungry Roman army, Durobrivae continued to change. This chapter considers the changes that the town went through in the late Roman period, and how it, the surrounding countryside and the industries which formed a part of that landscape, adapted to changing circumstances.

Firstly, let's summarise the state of the town and hinterland in the second century. Durobrivae, as yet unwalled, was expanding rapidly, and at its heart were a sequence of significant public buildings. We are not entirely sure of the functions of these buildings as they have not been excavated, but from their ground plans we can judge their likely functions. One was perhaps a *forum*, a market place; and the second a *mansio*, an official stop on the imperial post system. Such structures will have been paid for by the local elites, doing so to bring glory to their town, and the continued development of Durobrivae was reliant upon the continued interest of an essentially rural elite in an urban centre.

Looking out into the countryside, we can see that by this point the landscape in the Silt Fens was fully developed. What we must remember about this area is that it was essentially uninhabited at the point of the Roman Conquest. The fully developed landscape of the late second century, crowded with settlements, busy with activity, was a product almost entirely of the late first and early second centuries. It was a manifestation of the 'industrialisation' of salt production, an organised expanse of settlement dedicated to producing salt for the army, and salted meat. A little to the south were the Central Fens where there had been Iron Age occupation, but this had, by the second century, developed well beyond what it had been before the Conquest. Settlement had spread far from the Fenland islands, out over the Fens themselves, and along local communication ways (roads and canals). This area had, in the Iron Age, been under the control of the Iceni, but following the Icenian revolt it had been transferred to the control of the Corieltauvi, a move that ultimately placed it in the hinterland of Durobrivae. This was probably done because the Romans, seeing the valuable salt-production industry of the Central Fens, wanted to place it in the hands of a more 'reliable' tribe than the Iceni, following their revolt. Both of these areas, the Silt Fens and Fen islands, were connected to the 'mainland', and to the town towards which they looked economically, by a system of roads and canals, many of which were susceptible to local flooding but which, at great effort and frequent rebuildings, were maintained by the authorities.

To the west of the town the landscape had also developed, and for similar reasons. There is little trace of a pre-Roman pottery industry in the Nene Valley, though there may have been an iron-working industry on a small scale. So again the Romans may have been attracted to this area by the presence of natural resources made obvious by small-scale Iron Age activity. The authorities expanded the iron industry as they did with salt production in the Fens, developing local capacity to help meet the needs of the military. The pottery industry which grew up in the second century did so, perhaps, to take advantage of existing links with the army forged through iron and salt – the local elites seizing an opportunity to make more money out of their contracts to supply the state by increasing the range of goods on offer. As the money from army supply increased, the elites who controlled such trades were able to construct increasingly palatial residences in the Nene Valley. These structures were to undergo further change as the landscape, and the social relationships that structured it, evolved in the late Roman period.

Looking at the town itself, we followed it as it grew from an initial military presence, through small beginnings to a rapidly developing urban centre. The money from army contracts, flowing in quantities sufficient to allow the building of villas, perhaps even underpinned the building of the town. The same group of people paying for the villas also paid, in large part, for the key buildings, like the *forum*. But things were to change in the late Roman period.

First, let us consider the industries, the beginnings and evolution of which we have already followed. We will start with the salt industry, and the Fenland that supported it. Detailed analysis of this area has revealed that occupation was not static, and it has been suggested in Chapter Four that a kin-based social structure, where a family held land in common, rather than as individual holdings, dominated this landscape *(75)*. Thus, as the next generation grew up within this social structure, instead of waiting to inherit their parents' farm they would build another farm for themselves, but continue to share the 'common' family land.

104 Continuous maintenance of features like this dyke was crucial to the continued occupation of the Fens during the late Roman period

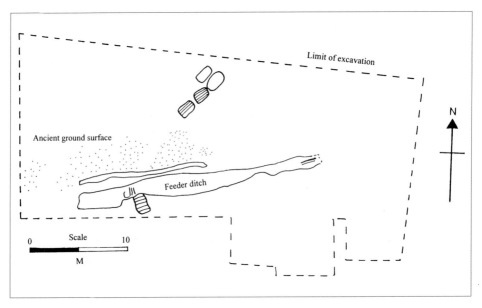

105 Plan of a late Roman salt-working area at Droitwich. Compare this plan to *71*, a traditional saltern. Wooden barrels have here replaced the settlement tanks. *After Woodiwiss 1992*

When the parents died, their farm buildings, instead of being taken on by the next generation, would fall into disuse. This meant that individual settlements were never long-term, lasting only about a generation before they were abandoned. It would also mean that settlement might shift naturally over time, a factor that becomes increasingly important as the water level began to rise in the late Roman period. The constantly shifting nature of this settlement pattern meant that the landscape was able to adapt as some areas became too wet to sustain occupation. As settlements only lasted a generation, when the time came for it to be naturally abandoned, that area would simply not be reoccupied. Settlement thus retreated naturally over time to the slightly higher ground to the north and the east, something which had serious implications for the later salt-making industry.

The evidence for late Roman salt making is difficult to interpret. We know that early salt-making methods involved the use of heavy terracotta trays which left clear archaeological traces – principally the material known as briquetage. In general, this makes it relatively easy to identify salt-production sites, as we encounter large amounts of broken salt containers, and various other archaeological remains. But in trying to specifically identify the late industry, we face two problems, one related to dating, the second to a possible change in salt-production technology. Generally, saltern sites are hard to date, because the debris that identifies them as salterns, the briquetage, is only rarely mixed with debris from substantial occupation. This makes sense, as salterns are not pleasant places, and people will tend to live at a distance from them if they can. The chief tool for dating sites in archaeology is pottery, which tends to be only present where it is being used, i.e. where people live. Thus, there is very little pottery on saltern sites, and we are robbed of our chief method of dating them.

However, we do know that the saltern sites where briquetage is in evidence tend to be early, say, for example, in the first half of the Roman occupation. What happened to salt production in the late Roman period? It is unlikely that a major industry, key to army supply, producing a very valuable commodity, and well-developed in early Roman Britain, simply ceased to exist. But, if salt production continued, why was it no longer visible? There appears to be a change of technology in the mid-Roman period – a change which explains the disappearance of briquetage for sites where salt may still have been produced.

At Nantwich in Cheshire, salt was a major industry in the Roman period. Here, however, unlike on the coastal sites, it was mined rather than produced from brine. However, evaporation techniques were still used to purify the salt, and indeed, in the early period of this industry, briquetage technology was used. However, this technology was replaced in the mid-Roman period by something which, in most circumstances, would leave very little archaeological trace. At Nantwich, in the late Roman period, salt seems to have been evaporated using wooden barrels set into pits in the ground instead of the settlement tanks used in earlier salterns, like those already noted in the Fens *(105)*. If this happened across the salt-production industry in Britain it would explain why there is very little late Roman briquetage. It was simply no longer in use. But it would also explain why there is very little archaeological trace of a salt industry at all. The containers in which the salt was produced and then traded were perishable, and would not be preserved, except in rare conditions. It might well be the case, then, that the late Roman salt-production industry switched to using wooden barrels as evaporation containers, and thus effectively vanished from the archaeological record, if not from the economy of the province.

Where does this leave us with our consideration of the late Roman landscape in the Silt Fens? This landscape was still inhabited, though under threat by rising waters. The real flooding problems seem to have come not from the sea, but from the fresh water which flowed through the Fens, carried by the rivers which run across the Fenland basin and into the Wash. The increased amount of water backing up on the landward side of the Silt Fens seems to have encouraged the spread of peat, the less inhabitable element of the Fenland landscape. But the other consequence of this would be the necessary retreat seaward of any salt-making community which was dependent upon brine. The more the fresh water backed up, and the more the peat spread, the less far inland briny salt water would have penetrated. This is doubtless one of the explanations for the shift of settlement towards the north-eastern part of the Fens during the Roman period – the inhabitants of the Fens, still making salt, though now in a less archaeologically visible way, were 'following' the brine required to keep their industry alive.

A significant issue that we need to consider here is that of the third-century floods. It has long been suggested in the traditional accounts of this region that in

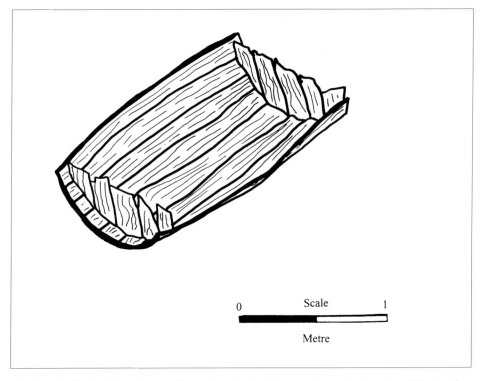

0   Scale   1

Metre

*106 Detail of a barrel used as a settling tank at the late Roman salt-production site of Droitwich.
After Woodiwiss 1992*

the mid-third century much of the landscape was inundated by large-scale flooding. This was caused, it has been suggested, by the fact that the civil wars that raged in the empire at this time had absorbed the attention of Britain's rulers. From AD 260–273 Britain was part of a secessionist portion of the western empire, the Imperium Galliarum divorced from central control, and under the leadership of its own sequence of rulers. These rulers, also responsible for Roman provinces in Spain, Gaul and Germany, stripped the British provinces of resources (both in terms of money and manpower), to fight wars on the continent, essentially leaving Britain to fend for itself. This drawing off of money and manpower led to shortages of both within Britain, and this may have had a great impact upon infrastructure maintained by the state. The moist obvious consequence would have been a failure to maintain the dyke systems which kept the Fens drained, but manpower from Fenland farms may also have been stripped away to serve the interests of the Gallic empire elsewhere. This lack of maintenance would, the theory goes, have led to widespread flooding, and the need to abandon large areas of otherwise productive land.

However, the issue of this 'flooding episode' is more complicated than it may at first appear. There is certainly evidence for flooding on many sites. We can see major flood incidents on sections of the Fen Causeway. A settlement excavated at

Throkenhalt, in the Silt Fens, seems to have declined in the third century due to flooding, and we even see flooding on the Fen islands to the south. But the precise dating of flood events is notoriously difficult, and it is certainly not possible to date them so precisely across different and widely spaced sites to be able to demonstrate that these instances belonged to the same episode. The best that we might be able to say is that perhaps flooding had become generally more common in the third and fourth centuries. This opens up the possibility that some of the flooding that we see on sites in the Silt Fens (for example, Throkenhalt) may not be flooding at all, but may be indicative of the natural functioning of the area's social structure, explored in Chapter Four. If the social nature of the settlement in this area, i.e. the shifting kin-based structure which meant that the next generation founded a new settlement on the edge of commonly-held land (rather than waiting to 'inherit' a specific farm), meant that settlements lasted for only a generation, the numbers of settlements failing in the landscape would be large, but it would be matched by large numbers of settlements being founded. Examples such as Throkenhalt Farm, then, may not be evidence for biblical-style floods, but the natural working of a landscape created by a kinship-based social structure, combined with low-lying Fenland topography. The site, abandoned naturally, would then have gradually silted up following abandonment – with no one keeping local groundwater under control through drainage. When excavated, this may well have looked like the site was abandoned due to flooding, whereas in fact it flooded *because* it was abandoned.

In the Central Fens, settlement was based on the islands, and was less precarious than that of the silts. The factors helping to curtail salt production in the silts would, of course, also effect this area, but the greater security from potential flooding problems gained by living on the gravel islands of this region allowed the maintenance of substantial settlements here. However, one important change did occur in the settlement pattern. The great tower at Stonea Grange, the suggested heart of the administration of this area, was gone, dismantled at the end of the second century. What does this suggest? It might be that the declining fortunes of the area had made it less important for the authorities to maintain a base here, or that the reason for the construction of the tower (to provide close administration of an area which had been in rebellion), was no longer significant enough to justify the expense. It may have been the case that, with the memory of the rebellion in the distance, and the area in decline, the tower was withdrawn.

The economy of the area may well have been in serious decline as well. The islands had been an advantage in the early Roman period as they were areas of stable ground where settlements could easily be built. But they were perhaps a disadvantage now *(107)*. Secure on their islands, the local inhabitants were less free to move their settlements to follow the brine as their northern counterparts. As the fresh water rose around the islands, diluting any brine that made its way in from the sea, salterns would have failed, and the salt industry would have become progressively untenable. By the late Roman period, perhaps only salterns in the north of the Central Fen area, near the Welney inlet, or on a major watercourse like the Nene would still have been able to function. This decline in the key wealth-producing industry of the area would have reduced its significance for the authorities in Durobrivae, and the Central Fens seem to have settled into quiet decline.

If we have a clear picture of the Fens, what about the western part of the hinterland of Durobrivae? We can start by looking at the fate of the industries in this area. Physically, the pottery industry remained centred on Sibson, to the west of the town, perhaps also with a subsidiary centre at Stanground, on the west. Grey ware (the more 'utilitarian' products of the industry) were produced in a conservative range of forms during the early phase of Nene Valley ware, and this remained the case in the later period. Yet, in terms of the production of colour-coated fine wares, during the early phase of Nene Valley ware there had been a massive explosion of what was available. The Nene Valley repertoire was wide, providing the local inhabitants with the full range of Roman-style pottery, including some elements, like platters (large plates, probably used for serving) that people in the region would not have been used to. But by the third century the pottery that was available became dominated by beakers. The early period, with many forms, was in a sense a period of experimentation which failed – people might have been interested in the new vessels at first, perhaps from a sense of novelty, but the interest did not last. Nevertheless, demand for this pottery, as in the early period, was supported by a strong connection with the army. As already noted, large quantities of late Nene Valley ware have been recovered from a range of sites on Hadrian's Wall, and even as far north as the southern shores of the Firth of Forth in Scotland. This probably represents a continuation of the piggy-backing of pottery onto bulk shipments of staple goods to the army from the region around Durobrivae.

So by the late Roman period the pottery industry was well established down the Nene Valley and along the river to the west and north of the town, and a stable but limited repertoire of pottery was being produced. But even in this later period the volume of production, measured by the number of kilns in operation, was increasing, and during this phase the Nene Valley industry had become one of the largest potteries that Roman Britain ever saw. This was presumably driven by the same factors underlying the unusually strong industrial development of other elements of the economy in this area – well-established estates, run by a local elite willing to engage with the imperial authorities in order to make money, and real opportunities to earn that wealth, created by fortuitous links with the Roman military supply network.

Iron production in the East Midlands also continued to expand into the late Roman period. Although the research that has so far been conducted still leaves us with only an outline understanding of the way the industry as a whole worked, we have sufficient evidence to know that the scale of production seems to have increased in the third and perhaps fourth centuries. In addition, new types of

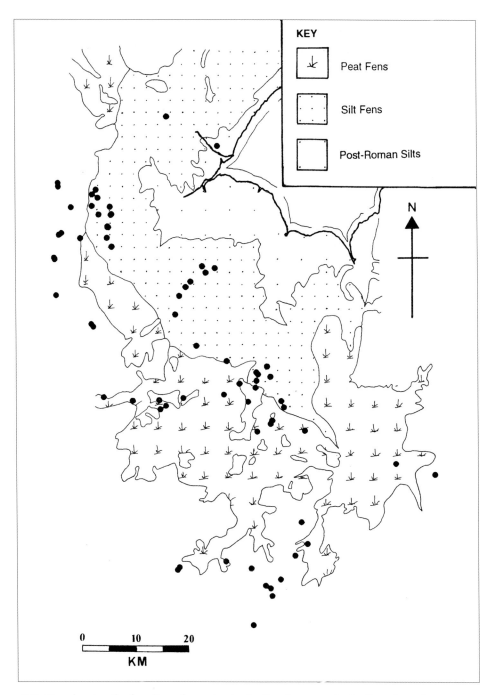

KEY

Peat Fens

Silt Fens

Post-Roman Silts

N

0   10   20
KM

107 Map showing the founding of new sites in the fourth century in the Fens. It can be seen that there are still sites being founded on and around the Central Fen islands, and in some parts of the Silts

technology were also being introduced (like, for example, more efficient types of furnace), which allowed the intensification of exploitation of local iron stone. In terms of the administrative organisation of the industry little seems to change from the early period, with large numbers of sites operating small-scale furnaces and occasional sites operating at greater levels of intensity. Production sites, where the ore was processed in furnaces, remained close to mining sites where the iron stone was actually mined. There is little information about how the iron-production sites fared at the end of the occupation – it is possible that the industry never completely failed, even with the collapse of the province, as small-scale working is known in the area from the Anglo-Saxon period, with growing importance again in the medieval and early modern periods.

There remains the mosaic school, focused upon Durobrivae *(108)*. We know little about this industry as it has never been studied in depth, and we can say little more than that it existed and that its probable focus was the town. Mosaics of a specific style are scattered across the eastern part of England, and as the distribution of mosaics attributed to the school clearly shows, they cluster in and around the territory of the town, suggesting that the craftsmen involved served the large and wealthy estates in the region. However, we must recognise the essential difference between the mosaic school and the other industries that we have looked at, like salt production, iron working or pottery. The main industries of the region were based upon making money from army-supply contracts, and supplying the needs of the estates as working economic entities. The mosaic school was essentially a luxury industry that grew up to service the needs of the province's super rich – the villa inhabitants. The mosaic industry was, in effect, about spending the wealth that other industries created, and providing a luxury. The fact that such an industry seems to be based upon the town, and that it was not part of the money-making enterprises of the estates themselves, might even indicate that, unlike the other industries, those who practised this activity were independent of the villa owners, a group of independent craftsmen, based in the town, offering their services to the rich of the region. They were perhaps attracted to Durobrivae precisely because those with money in the area were unusually wealthy, and had money to spend on non-essentials like mosaics.

We should not forget the principal occupation of the majority of the populace – agriculture. Sites like Orton Hall Farm continued to develop in the late Roman period *(109)*, perhaps tied into the estate system, still clinging on as independent farms (though as we shall see this becomes less likely as the late period wears on). It is sites like this, however, that produced the agricultural surplus that allowed villa complexes and the town to survive, as without food arriving in the town every day it would have quickly failed. Cereal cultivation must have been important, as stone-built corn dryers (like those found, for example, at Site 2 at Lynch Farm), used for processing cereals and possibly involved in the production of beer, become increasingly common. Animal husbandry (perhaps particularly on the Fenland side of the town, intermingled with salt-production sites as discussed in

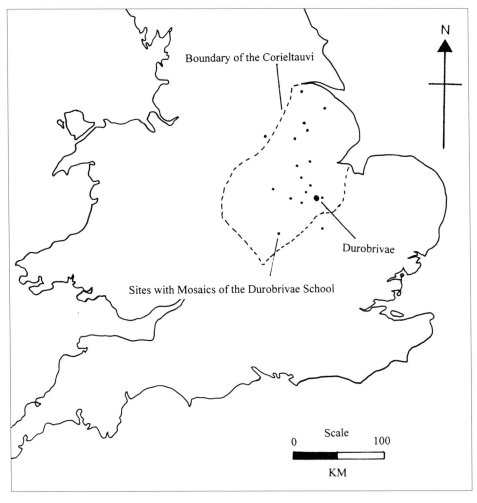

108 A map showing the different locations of the known mosaics associated with the Durobrivae School

Chapters Three and Four) must also have been a key farming activity. The detailed excavation and analysis of the site at Orton Hall Farm provides us with what is probably our most complete picture of a working farm from this, or any other period, from within the hinterland of the town, and here the excavator notes that a possible mill house would have produced large amounts of flour – too great to be consumed on site. There also appears to be expanded accommodation, higher volumes of brewing being conducted, and provision for greatly increased numbers of stock animals. The farm thus seems to have been geared up to higher volumes of production of various kinds of produce, possibly reflecting the fact that the farm had passed into imperial control, and become state property – the suggestion being that these extra supplies were perhaps destined for the army. This is difficult to say with any certainty, but what Orton Hall Farm suggests is that farming as an activity

139

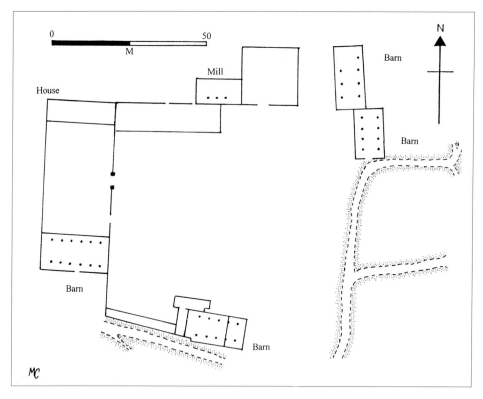

109 A plan of the site of Orton Hall Farm, a large farm to the south-east of Durobrivae, possibly involved in its later history in producing supplies for the army. *After Jones and Mattingly, 1990. Illustration by Melanie Cameron*

may have had as strong a connection with the military as the other activities carried on around the town – and that whatever the form of those connections, it was ultimately the demands of the military that once again supported an artificially large market for commodities of whatever kind produced in the area.

This leaves the town itself. Even without detailed excavation evidence it is possible, as illustrated in Chapter Two, to generate an outline history of the urban centre. What little we do know is interesting, and becomes meaningful when we have an understanding of wider events in the hinterland. By the end of the second century the core buildings of the town had been developed, and the suburbs had grown. We also know from aerial photographs that a town wall was constructed sometime after the second century. Most other walled towns in Britain acquired their circuit of defences mid-third century, more, perhaps, as a civic elaboration than from any feeling that the town needed to be defended – this structure at Durobrivae should probably be dated, then, to the same period. However, as the later Roman period progressed, we see signs of decline. The suburbs of the town appear to contract and domestic buildings within the walls are progressively abandoned. Many of these are the high-status urban houses which we have postulated were owned by those who had built the villas in Nene Valley. This leaves us with an apparent contradiction, with the town itself in decline at the point at which associated industries are well established. The villas themselves, as we shall see, were actually expanding during this period and entering their heyday.

What impact does this have upon our understanding of the villas, and their development? By the late Roman period some of these structures were of immense size – so large that one such site, excavated by Artis under the villages of Castor and Ailsworth, is indeed palatial in scale and has been considered as a possible palace by Mackreth *(101)*. He suggests that it may be the seat of a late provincial governor, or even the residence of the 'Duke of the Saxon Shore' with responsibility for the defence of the east of England and perhaps the administration of the Fens as well. This suggestion emerges from the possibility that the Fens were a single estate in need of a unified administration, which we have already discounted, but does serve to illustrate the scale of some of the private villas in the area, and gives a hint at the underlying wealth which must have been present to support such establishments. We have considered the clear strength of the economy of the region in this late period, industry by industry, but the generally well-appointed and grandiose nature of the villas of the Nene Valley cannot simply be explained by vague suggestions of industrial or economic wealth. How did the administrative, economic and social structures of the area combine to channel such wealth into the construction of villas?

A possible explanation is tied up with the state of the town and its connection to the industries at this period. It is a well-understood trend that the local elites in the Roman world, the mainstay of town financing in the early empire, retreated into the country during the later Roman period. Obligation piled onto obligation, and becoming active in town affairs became ever more onerous and expensive but less

110 A reconstruction of the Orton Hall Farm site as it may have looked in the late second century. Such buildings would have been relatively commonplace across the western (upland) part of the hinterland of the town. *Illustration by Melanie Cameron*

rewarding as the obvious and high-profile activities such as building new buildings that the town required were already done. All that remained were the less glamorous aspects of the ongoing life of a mature town, like repairs and running costs, and the elites progressively lost interest in the towns. Presumably Durobrivae and its ruling class were not exempt from this process, and we may postulate a decline in the vibrancy of civic life as the late Roman period progressed. This was not to say that the market centred on the town failed – we have no evidence that it did. The industries that used the town as a centre were flourishing, and so it seems reasonable that as a market centre the town remained at least reasonably buoyant.

In other aspects of town life, however, there is a more mixed picture. There were signs of decay, with significant contraction in the suburbs, but also some signs of continuing wealth. The Water Newton treasure (see cover illustration), a range of impressive and finely worked objects, many bearing Christian symbols, dates to this later period. The treasure is interpreted variously as the treasury of an early church, or at least a wealthy Christian. But the fact that Christians in Britain tended to be urban-based may explain its presence in a town where perhaps the traditional elite were withdrawing to their country estates, and were less prominent than they had been. Interestingly, this is a similar picture as that presented by the 'decline' of Stonea, the possible centre of authority in the Central Fens. The tower was now gone but the market was still in place – visible signs of control from the elite were fading as their interest was withdrawn, but life and the pursuit of wealth continued. We should not imagine, however, that this represents an impoverished region. As the town, and other centres like Stonea, declined, the villas flourished, as the money that might have been spent on the town was spent upon elaborating the country residences of the elites – buying, for example, mosaics from the Durobrivae School.

Although villas get larger in the Nene Valley area towards the end of the Roman occupation, they also seem to decrease in number. As one of the prime functions of a villa was to act as the centre of an estate, any reduction in the number of villas probably represents the failure of estates, and their subsequent acquisition by neighbours. The average size of an estate would thus have swollen in the late Roman period, something that may have led to increased self-sufficiency amongst the estates that survived. Self-sufficiency was always a goal for Roman landowners, and underpins a lot of ancient literature on agriculture and 'household management'. It is seen in the existing papers surviving from the Appianus estate in Egypt (the papers of which survive to give us a detailed picture of its workings), where we see the estate trying to supply its own needs wherever possible, and keep imports from the outside world to a minimum. We know that the super-rich landowners of Rome might ship goods from their estate holdings in Africa so that they did not have to buy in produce, for example, to feed workers in holdings in Italy.

This same process might be applied to the Durobrivae estates, albeit on a smaller scale. In the early period (first and second century), when the average size of estates was smaller, a single estate would have been unable to supply its own needs. It might have produced enough grain and pottery, but not, for example, metal work. This gap would have been made up by acquiring goods at the market. As the estates grew bigger, swallowing smaller competitors, this situation would have changed; the larger estates, supplying more of their own needs, would have less need of imports, thus reducing trade through the town. There would always have been some trade in the town, and as we shall see in the next chapter, there is some evidence that the town responded to this situation by engaging in new activities, so the market would have remained active. But this model helps us to explain the more generalised decline of the town at the very time that we see the rise of very ornate late Roman villas.

Another activity may have helped to keep the civic functions of the town alive – that of tax collection. Driven by the steady erosion of the value of Roman currency due to inflation, a major change occurred to the nature of Roman taxation, perhaps dating to the third century – tax began to be collected more commonly in kind. The *annonae* (tax in kind) may actually have come to substitute all or large parts of the collection of taxation in coin. In practice this made what was collected much less portable – a collection of tax in kind infers a system of local collection points to gather what is owed, and perhaps to process it to allow it to meet state needs. Although collection was the responsibility of an official appointed by the *civitas,* officials working under him would probably have operated at various locations and an obvious candidate for one such location would, of course, be Durobrivae. As the civic functions of the town as a local trading and administrative centre declined, its official role in life of the region may have been, to a degree, supported by its role as a local tax-collection centre. At the very least this new function would have ensured a high degree of through traffic and activity. The late Roman period, then, was a time of mixed fortunes across the town and its surrounding territory, some aspects of which were in decline, whilst others were actually expanding, the villas themselves imposing structures like never before.

How then might this landscape have looked? Our travelling pot salesman would, of course, be long dead, but perhaps his descendants still travelled these roads. The stretches of wet, reedy Fen between the mainland and the settlements out on the Silts would be wider by the late Roman period. The roads, much repaired, and raised time and time again to try and overcome problems of flooding, must have had a somewhat makeshift and patched feel by this time. Many of the canals in use in the early and mid-Roman period were silted and disused by now. Much was waterlogged and overgrown. Near the end of his journey, any traveller would be passing through areas which were once inhabited, and now abandoned. Wooden structures, with walls of wattle, would deteriorate quickly in this environment, but perhaps a few uprights, parts of old walls or collapsed piles of daub were still visible where there had once been farms. Lines of reeds would now be growing where there had once been drainage ditches. Further into the Fens,

111 Reconstruction of the Fenland landscape of the late Roman period. Note the patched nature of the road, and the abandoned settlement. Some occupation continues, but it is now far into the Fen, close to the coast where there is still brine for salt production. *Illustration by Melanie Cameron*

however, there were still the columns of smoke rising into the air. The communities were shrunken now, and not so much salt flowed along this road as had once done so, but salters were still at work, now boiling out salt in barrels which were periodically transported to distant Durobrivae.

The situation was similar, if not identical, down in the Central Fens and on the Fen islands. Here occupation had always been on solid ground, and the rise in the water levels, although affecting some of the lower-lying homes, would not have ended all settlement. The Fen Causeway, like the roads to the north, now much patched and raised against the waters, still ran through this area, connecting the people here to the outside world. The settlement at Stonea was still there, still perhaps with a market being held, but at its heart was a large,empty space, strewn with rubble, where the tower had once stood. As with the Fens, salt and meat was still traded out of the area, down the road to Durobrivae, but what had once been a flood of goods was now little more than a trickle. The rising water was fresh, run-off from the uplands, and the salting industry, with no brine, was all but gone.

The landscape to the west of the town was, perhaps, not so different as it had been, though with fewer villas, and those that now looked down into the valley from the higher ground were larger than they had been, with ornate façades. Between these 'super-villas' were the remains of smaller residences, now abandoned, or perhaps turned over to squatters, and low-level industrial uses – these were less rich now, but those that survived were very rich indeed, living on self-contained, self-supporting estates, and were rarely seen outside their villa complexes. Town life had dwindled – the wealthy rarely went there now, but even so Durobrivae was far from deserted. Craftsmen and small independent traders still carried on business there, and government officials still called. Every once in a while the town was thronging – huge herds of cattle and piles of produce were collected on the market square. A century before such a scene would have been the sign of a healthy market day, but now it meant that it was a day to pay taxes.

7

THE END OF THE TOWN

With the end of Roman rule at the beginning of the fifth century, the social and economic structures of the province failed. The end of Roman Britain is a difficult period to study, with great changes, but little evidence to help us understand them. The traditional date for the Roman withdrawal from Britain is AD 410, when troops were stripped from the province to fight in the civil wars that convulsed the empire, and we do appear to see a very rapid collapse of Roman-style culture in the early fifth century. We have an image, strengthened by this single date of AD 410, of the Romans leaving the province, and taking with them all concept of order and civilisation, almost as though the tap of 'Roman culture' had suddenly been turned off. However, there is another way of understanding the early fifth century – that the withdrawal of Roman rule was principally a political rather than a cultural event. What this would suggest is that the cultural changes which we have already seen in the later Roman period led naturally to the post-Roman situation. The political events focused around the withdrawal of Roman power may well have accelerated existing cultural trends, but the seeds of post-Roman Britain should be discernible in the landscape of late Roman Britain.

Roman pottery production in the Nene Valley seems to come to an end, at the latest, by the first quarter of the fifth century (c.AD 420). The Fens were rapidly abandoned, bringing a swift end to any salt production still being carried out, and the town itself dwindled, and finally failed. The fate of the villas is unclear, due to a lack of any large-scale excavation, but at many of the large Nene Valley sites like Bancroft or Sacrewell there seems to be a period of late Roman decline, sites falling into disuse at, or soon after, the end of the occupation. By contrast, at Orton Hall Farm, we see possible mingling of Roman and Anglo-Saxon pottery in the final phases of the Roman occupation, and the excavator suggests that the farm was handed over to Anglo-Saxons as a going concern, even before the end of the province. The site certainly continued to be occupied into the post-Roman period. The general picture, then, seems to be one of very rapid disintegration of institutions, industries and social structure, perhaps with a few scattered survivals. Very quickly, as the fifth century wore on, a region that had appeared wealthy and vibrant only a few decades before was home only to small farmsteads and the ruins of the town and villas. Why did Durobrivae and its hinterland ultimately prove to be so fragile?

The first question that we need to ask is: was the decline of Roman Britain in general, and the region around the town in particular, all it seems? The answer to this is possibly not. Some commentators see the end of Roman Britain more as a transitional phase, perhaps beginning in the third century, in which the villa economy of the Roman province gradually changes. By AD 700–750 an early feudal landscape begins to emerge, but as the result of transformation of the Roman province, not necessarily its total destruction. In this model, although many of the physical structures of the empire fail in the fifth century, many of the social structures, at least in a localised way, live on. The suggestion, in effect, is that the villa estates clung on, even though the towns had vanished, and even though the actual physical structure of villas at their heart could no longer be maintained. Despite physical decline the bonds that bound the peasantry to the local elites continued. Such a situation is difficult to see – it was a period when there was little activity that left significant archaeological traces, but this does not mean that social structures of this kind did not exist. The emergence in the early medieval period of elites, may simply be a sign that they were becoming archaeologically visible again, as activity that left archaeological traces began to increase. Does this theory make sense of any of the limited evidence that we have from the area of Durobrivae?

The first step is to examine the actual evidence of abandonment that we have *(112)*, and in examining the situation in more detail we will start with the town. The difficulty from this perspective is that, as with almost every period of the town's development, the main evidence comes from the suburbs, and whereas with other periods we have the crop marks from within the defences to guide us about what might be happening in the town's heart, what we really want to know for the town's final phase is when were the central areas abandoned? The crop marks alone cannot tell us this. What the excavations in the suburbs do indicate is that the outlying areas of the town, north and south, were largely empty by the later part of the fourth century. It is logical that these, the outlying areas that contained none of the vital institutions of the town, would have been the first to be abandoned as the town began to shrink. This shrinkage, taking place before the Roman withdrawal from the province was part of other, independent, trends which were tending towards urban decline in the later Roman period, and these have been discussed in Chapter Six. But what it does tell us is that the town of the very early fifth century was a shrunken version of its earlier self – the vital economic life of the second and third centuries now a memory. The town, then, relied absolutely upon its core institutions to stay in existence as a town – its identity as an urban centre depended not upon qualities intrinsic to the settlement,

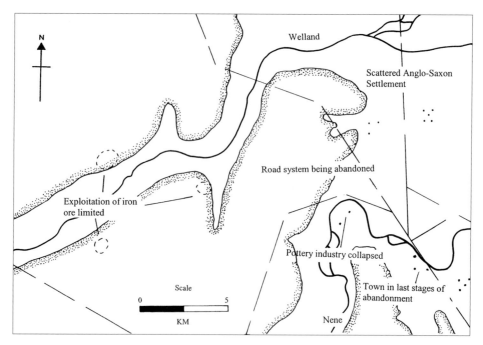

112 Generalised map of the western part of Durobrivae's hinterland in the early to mid-fifth century

but the role that it was given by higher authorities – upon functioning as a tax-collection site, an administrative post, or a stopping-place on the imperial post system. The town, in effect, had become less important to the day-to-day lives of people around it than it had been. The populace was now much more focused upon the estates, either as craftsmen that produced goods for the estate economy, or as workers on the land, tied to the estates through early forms of feudal serfdom. Such a decline in relevance, of course, is reflected in the physical shrinking of the town. The consequences for Durobrivae of the withdrawal of the central authority, the effective collapse of the province as a centralised governmental unit, are extreme and obvious. With no real function for those that lived around it, and suddenly none of the central functions that the state had imparted to it, there was simply nothing left for the town to do. With the end of the province it had no role, and with the change rapid enough to prevent any attempt to reinvent itself, the town simply failed and was abandoned. Drastic as this may appear for the actual urban centre, this scenario opens up interesting possibilities for our consideration of the hinterland. If the town was relatively irrelevant for the population of the hinterland by AD 410, need its collapse necessarily have affected the way they lived their lives to any significant degree?

The first element of the hinterland to consider is the Fens. This area had been in apparent long-term decline since the third century. Out on the Silt Fens settlement had drifted, shifting to the north and the east, whilst the total number of settlements declined. By the end of the Roman occupation large areas to the south and west of the Silt Fens must have been either completely abandoned, or at the least very sparsely populated. Several reasons have been put forward for this decline: the apparent floods of the third century, the spread through the empire of the *agri deserti* (deserted lands) as the population of the empire declined, a decline of the salt-production industry that made living in the Fens less necessary, and generally rising water levels. The truth may be that some or all of these factors came into play to encourage a general decline in the number of people living out on the Fens. In general, though, settlement appears to have been contracting back towards pre-Roman areas of occupation since well before the actual end of the Roman occupation.

There are important traces of post-Roman settlement in the Fens, though once again mostly concentrated on the Fen islands. In this southern area of the Fenland, around the Fen islands of March and Stonea, occupation outlived the province, possibly because settlements here were located on areas of higher ground, but also perhaps because it was an area that was well established, the ancient heart of Fenland, inhabited for many thousands of years. The excavations at the Stonea Grange site revealed traces of a number of sunken feature buildings, rectangular pits which formed the basis of Anglo-Saxon domestic buildings. A number of

113 The changing face of Fen drainage. Not only are dykes necessary to drain water, but steam-driven pumps were common in the nineteenth and early twentieth century, located in pump houses like the one in the centre of this picture. This is an artificial landscape, and without constant effort, it cannot survive. That is as true today as it was in the closing years of the Roman occupation

these Anglo-Saxon buildings were discovered built over and into the ruins of the Roman-period site, suggesting that even in the post-Roman period it may have remained a relatively large settlement. There are also indications of Anglo-Saxon settlement on Whittlesea island (someway to the west of the March and Stonea islands), so the continued settlement on Stonea was not an isolated instance.

The second broad element of the hinterland to consider is that of the western upland and the area of the Nene Valley itself. Farming, despite the focus upon the 'hard' archaeological evidence of the town itself, its villas and industry, was the occupation of the vast majority of the inhabitants of the region. Agriculture was, of course, based around the villa estates. The estates managed the production of its tenants, organising the collection and sale of surplus. But with the collapse of the provincial government, and the vanishing of the town, what happened to the farmers? The first thing that we can be fairly sure of is that, whilst there was still occupation, there was still farming – people, after all, always need to eat. The collapse of wider provincial structures, or even the estates themselves, will have had no impact upon the need of the population to continue feeding themselves. The evidence that we have for the immediate post-Roman period does give us indications of continued occupation. We have already seen in the Fens that, even with wide-scale abandonment of the landscape at large, there were still people living at Stonea, and on other islands, after the end of the province. We know from excavation that at Orton Hall Farm a sizeable establishment seems to have passed into the hands of Anglo-Saxons as a going concern at some point in the late Roman period, and occupation continued once the province had collapsed *(114)*. We do not have the evidence to say whether or not this was a widespread pattern of events as the Roman period came to a close, but if, as we have suggested, the town had become largely irrelevant to the lives of people in the hinterland by the point of the provincial collapse, the vanishing of the town in the early fifth century would have left the tenants of the estates to continue farming, quite possibly with only limited effect upon their lives. The real issue for these farmers would have been what happened to the villa estate structure of the rural economy – what happened to the inhabitants of the villas, their landlords, and quite possibly their 'feudal lords'. This we will consider a little later in this chapter, after first looking at the fate of the final aspect of the region, the industries.

The principal industries of the area, salt and pottery production, and the mining and processing of iron, do largely seem to end with the end of the province. How, and why, did these falter? The salt-production industry seems already to have been in decline. Given the fact that settlement appears to have been shifting away from the areas where salterns were traditionally concentrated, it may be that environ-mental changes had affected the viability of the industry. Salt production relies upon a steady supply of brine (salt water), which entered the Silt Fens via tidal creeks reaching in from the Wash. But they must also be located near to a source of fuel; in the case of the Fenland salterns this was almost certainly peat. This means that the salterns were located not on the coast, as might be expected, but further inland,

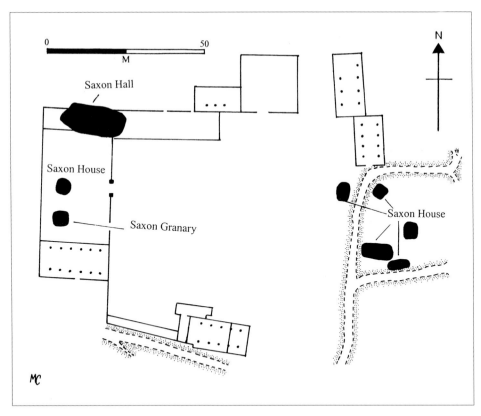

114 The Saxon buildings at Orton Hall Farm. *After Jones and Mattingly, 1990. Illustration by Melanie Cameron*

on, or close to, the junction between peat and silt. Peat, however, is a characteristic of fresh water logging; it is an indication of water flowing from inland, down rivers and streams, and collecting in an area where it has become trapped. This freshwater flow seems to have been heavy with silt brought from upland areas, silt which was deposited as the fresh water hit the salt water of the sea (a process called solifluc-tion). This continual deposition of silt led to the creations of the Silt Fens, but also encouraged the silting up of the very rivers carrying the freshwater out to the Wash, and which filled with brine at high tide. This had two effects – it made it harder for freshwater, pooling behind the great silt barrier of the Silt Fens, to escape out to sea (thus encouraging the spread of the Peat Fen), but it also interrupted the supply of brine flowing in to the saltern fields. Analysis of the settlement pattern has shown, however, that the north-east section of the Silt Fens was still a viable part of the settlement pattern in the late Roman period. It was still playing its part in the local estate-based economy, even if to a reduced extent compared to previous centuries. The failure of the estate would, however, have been the final blow to the area, and with environmental conditions degenerating, and the market for salt gone, settlement too must have soon dwindled.

What about events in the other industries? We know that pottery production in the Nene Valley ended relatively rapidly after the end of the provincial authority, perhaps continuing to AD 420. The industry was producing a simplified repertoire by the end of the Roman period, some 'Samian' replacement, but largely colour-coated beakers, jugs, bowls and dishes, alongside standard production of storage jars. This level of production seems to have continued right until the end of the industry, but actual events as the pottery kilns ceased production are, as usual with this period, obscure. There is, however, one site, that of Orton Hall Farm, where we have a small clue as to what the situation on the very eve of the collapse of the industry may have been.

A single sherd of Anglo-Saxon pottery was discovered during the excavation of this site. The interesting thing about this sherd is that it was discovered in a context where it was associated with objects (including pottery) of a definitely late Roman nature. What can this sherd tell us about the state of the ceramics industry in the closing years of Roman rule? It is, after all, only one sherd. The significance of this small scrap of pottery is that it shows us that, on at least this site in the closing years of the occupation, a different kind of pottery was being produced and was in circulation at the same time that the Nene Valley industry was still producing. The excavator suggests that this indicates that, even before the end of Roman Britain, property and land were being handed over to the Anglo-Saxon 'immigrants'. This may have been property that belonged to the central authorities of the province, being awarded as gifts to these incomers for their services (probability military in nature) to the imperial government. What this might hint at, though we must again remind ourselves that it is only one sherd, is that even as the central authority was collapsing, some elements of the existing population, or incoming individuals from outside the province, were establishing a different style of pottery, hand-made, and cruder, not sourced from the Nene Valley kilns. If the people who made the pot from which this sherd came were incomers, it might also hint that the imperial authorities were introducing a new factor into the region. It might be an indication that German colonists were being settled upon imperial land, something which might have begun to challenge the existing estate structure. Suddenly there were properties, not controlled by the great estates, and inhabited by people with little or no relationship to the traditional structures of authority in the area.

What significance does this have to the wider fate of the pottery industry? Like the salt industry, the pottery industry relied upon two things: the villa estate structures, and, more indirectly, regional links with the Roman army. The collapse of the links with the army will have robbed the Nene Valley producers (and, of course, the villa owners that controlled them), of a large export market – the ability to send pottery over long distances at the army's expense. The scale of the industry could not be supported without such an essentially artificial arrangement, as pottery, being both bulky and fragile, was not capable of commanding significant markets over long distances in the ancient world when subsidised transport was not being

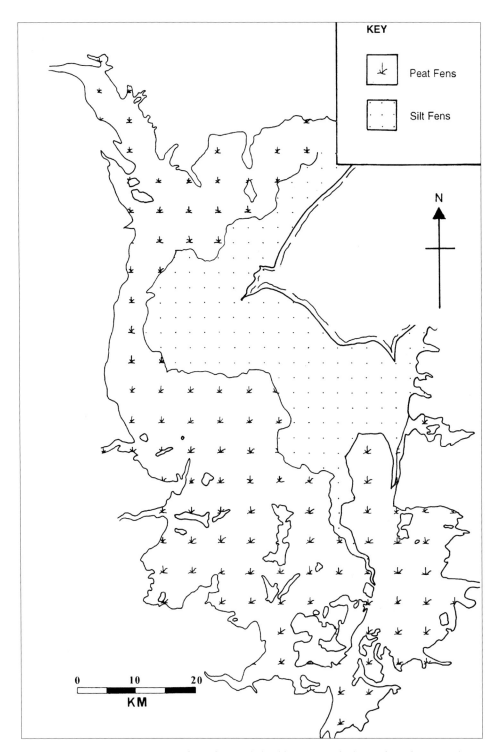

KEY

⊥ Peat Fens

∴ Silt Fens

N

0   10   20

KM

115 The post-Roman Fens. Note how the uninhabitable Peat Fen had spread north, encroaching upon the area of Roman settlement, and reducing the viability of the Roman salt-making industry. *After Waller, 1994*

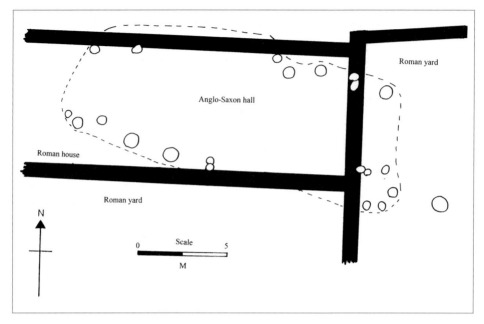

116 A detail from Orton Hall Farm, showing the Anglo-Saxon hall built over the site of the Roman house. After Mackreth, 1996

provided by the authorities. The remaining markets would therefore be the more local ones, particularly the 'captive audience' of the estate tenants. At one time this might have been enough, with a large population out in the Fens, to preserve some vestige of an industry. But with the Fens in sharp decline, that market was shrinking too. If the local estates were struggling to cope with losing their military market at the same time that their local market was shrinking, suddenly were also under pressure from incomers introducing a new style of pottery, the swift collapse of the Nene Valley pottery industry should come as little surprise.

What then, of the iron-production industry? If we are correct in assuming that, like the salt production and pottery production, the iron industry was essentially an estate-based form of production, controlled by the villa owners, traded through Durobrivae, and supported through a long-term military contract, the removal of those army contracts would also have drastically reduced the requirement for iron ore. Iron, along with salt, may well have been one of the bigger 'money spinners' for the estate elites, and with the army contracts no longer needing to be fulfilled, as with pottery, the only market available to sell the iron to would have been a strictly local one. Unlike the pottery industry, however, which produces a finished 'product', iron is a raw material, and the incomers continued to need it, albeit in smaller quantities.

Finally, we should also consider the mosaic school based in the town. Although, as suggested in the previous chapter, by the end of the occupation it was the case that the town had already been in decline for some time, it may still have been the base for 'luxury' industries which specialised in serving the owners of the estates themselves – the principal archaeological evidence for this comes from the mosaic school. These tessellated and patterned floorings clearly required wealth, and the fate of this industry is thus intimately connected to the fate of the villa owners themselves. Without villa owners, and their patronage, there could be no mosaics. Did they survive the end of Roman Britain?

The villas that we see certainly seem to end at, or soon after, the end of the Roman occupation. There are, sadly, very few well-excavated examples of such sites from our area that would give us an idea about the end of the villas, but it is certain that these structures were economically dependent upon the estates that they ran. As the wider economy of the province collapsed, and the army contracts that had supported the estates for so many years lapsed, it seems that the villas fell into disrepair, and were abandoned. But the estates themselves are perhaps different, and it is certainly the case that the 'collapse' may have been less total than it at first appears. The fate of the estates (and those that owned them) is, in fact, the key to how we might understand the end of the Roman period in the hinterland of Durobrivae.

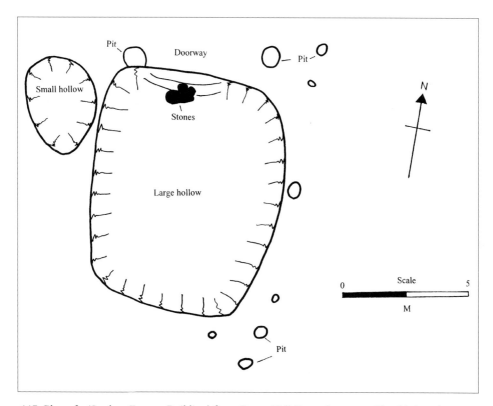

117 Plan of a 'Sunken Feature Building' from Orton Hall Farm. Structures like this have been found built into the Roman sites of Orton Hall Farm and Stonea Grange, but they have also been discovered near Empingham. *After Mackreth, 1996*

By the late Roman period we saw a situation where large estates dominated the landscape, having squeezed out their smaller rivals, and where a single estate might control enough resources to be almost self-sufficient. This reduced the role of the market in Durobrivae, as the estates were no longer trading as much with each other. The removal of central authority may have, in the short term, had little effect upon the estate structure. By this time the estates may have been very large indeed, and the 'tenants' living upon them be more like serfs. Once the provincial administration was gone the need to collect taxes and to maintain the town as an administrative centre will have ceased – with no tax for the provincial administration to collect, the prime remaining function of the town was gone. This might explain its apparent rapid abandonment in the years following AD 410, and may actually have represented a short-term benefit for the estates, freeing them of the obligation to pay tax.

The effect upon the estates, then, was to turn them into what were effectively independent fiefdoms, but a crucial difference will have been the sudden cessation of any contracts to supply the army. We know that the pottery industry supplied the army, so the sudden collapse when the army market was removed suggests that it was this that was key to keeping the industry viable. Without the money from the contracts with the army the estates would have been in trouble, but as the industry folded, much of what made these estates recognisable as 'Roman' in the archaeology would have vanished also. Without the wealth required to maintain them, even if they survived initially, the estates must have gradually broken down.

If the estate system, in the first instance, survived into the post-Roman periodand then unravelled, how can we model that disintegration in a way which makes sense of the events in this area in the fifth and sixth centuries? We know the general situation that the estates were in – the fact that this area was subject, in the aftermath to the collapse of Roman rule, to an influx of Angles and Saxons. This clearly didn't bode well for the long-term survival of the estate system, but not all of it will have collapsed at once. If the authority of any of the estates remained intact, and the control of one family over a work force on scattered farms survived, estates in some reduced form may have lingered on. However, with the Fens in decline, and any holdings east of the town rapidly being lost, such 'ghost estates' are unlikely to have generated much wealth. Not all estates will have had holdings spread evenly across the region – and those with a greater stake in the Fens than others may not have survived the loss of these areas as the Fens were abandoned. Estates that remained would simply have dwindled to agricultural 'fiefdoms' based, perhaps, around crumbling villas.

When this area was entered by the Anglo-Saxons, they may have encountered a patchwork of farming communities, some still organised along the lines of their old Roman estates. The industries were gone, as was the town itself, but the basic structure of the Roman countryside, albeit a denuded and threadbare remnant, may still have remained. It may well be this situation that we see at Orton Hall Farm *(116* and *118)*, where an Anglo-Saxon hall of some substance was built over

118 A Saxon hall building. This is the type of structure that may have been built into the ruins of Orton Hall Farm. *Illustration by Melanie Cameron*

the site of the original Roman house. The fragment of Anglo-Roman pottery found here, and considered earlier as possible evidence of Anglo-Saxon mercenaries being moved onto this farm in the closing years of the Roman administration, may actually represent something different. It is more than possible that it actually represents 'infiltration' as Anglo-Saxons moved into the gaps opening up in the fabric of Roman-British society as estates collapsed.

Was the Anglo-Saxon arrival the end of the story? It is possible that it was not. It becomes clear when comparing maps of settlement in different periods that some settlements survived and seem to form the basis for the landscape that emerged in the Middle Ages. This seems to be particularly the case with the settlements that ran along the Fen Edge, guarding access to the Fens themselves. These 'gateway' settlements emerge as villages in the Middle Ages, and still exist today.

8

THE FUNCTIONING WHOLE

We have seen Durobrivae rise and fall, and followed various elements of its hinterland as they grew and developed, stagnated and finally either ended along with the town, or survived it. Each of these elements is a different thread, and we must now gather those threads together to tell the complete story of Durobrivae, the Fenland town, and its hinterland.

Interpretation of the landscape of Roman Britain has tended to revolve around the essential division between the 'civilian' landscape of the south and east, and the 'military' landscape of the north and west. Some commentators have renamed the two landscape blocks 'native' (as opposed to military) and 'villa' (as opposed to civilian). This difference has also been thought of in terms of centralised (south-east) and decentralised (north-west) societies in late Iron Age Britain, and how this was reflected in the conquest of the province. The town and its hinterland are located in the 'villa' landscape, even though (as we have seen) much of it lacks villas.

The problem lies in the fact that this broad caricature of the landscape of Roman Britain, splitting the island into two big blocks of villa/non-villa scale is, of course, too simplistic, and the real situation was much more complex. Firstly, a common and recurring difficulty is defining what a villa actually is. The word 'villa' is a term which covers such a wide range of structures, ranging, in Britain, from small stone-built farmhouses of a few rooms to palaces like that at Fishbourne with great ranges of rooms and whole complexes of outbuildings. Several ways of subdividing the mass of 'villas' by establishing different categories for them have been tried, for example, by ground plan. Even so, comparison between a relatively modest site like Barton Court Farm, a large working agricultural site like Orton Hall Farm, well appointed houses like Woodchester and Great Witcombe, or the palace at Fishbourne, must lead us to question what factors actually link these five structures, each with different architectural pretensions and different functions, from farmstead to grand palatial residence. The term 'villa' thus remains problematic, and we need to bear this in mind as we consider various structures in the hinterland of Durobrivae.

Secondly, villas were not distributed evenly across the whole of this so-called 'villa' zone *(119)*. Basic distribution maps of villa-type sites illustrate the fact that there are significant gaps within the distribution of villas, large patches in the landscape where there are no villas at all. These gaps occur notably in large areas of Salisbury Plain, Sussex and Kent, and, of course, in the Fens. In the latter case the absence of villas has been considered by some as evidence that this land was an imperial estate. The second point to make is that villas were not the only structures in the rural landscape of Roman Britain. This may seem self-evident, but it is something that needs to be remembered when whole swathes of territory are characterised by reference to a single type of (elite) structure. The 'villa and village' complex at Stanwick, Northamptonshire, is an example of a more complex picture than a concentration simply on villa structures will allow. So when thinking about the 'villa' zone, we also need to think about farms and villages with a possible connection to the villas themselves, but also unconnected non-villa settlements in the same landscape. In the East Midlands we must contrast 'villas' and more substantial sites like Whitwell *(95)* and Empingham *(78)* with sites like Werrington, an Iron Age and Roman enclosure north of Peterborough, containing a small, simple building *(120)*. The variation between villas and sites like Werrington is a crucial aspect of the rural landscape, and is evident over even relatively small 'regional' landscapes. The simple 'dualistic' model of villa/non-villa can even be seen to break down at the level of individual sites. Both low-status (i.e. 'unromanised') structures and villas may occasionally be found together, representing different phases of the same site, or even different aspects of the same.

If the terms villa/non-villa tell us little, how do we begin to look at different types of site in the landscape? Rather than trying to sort such sites into artificial categories, a more profitable approach may be to rate the sites themselves on the basis of what is actually found on them. Instead, therefore, of trying to work out what type of building we are looking at, we might think of it in terms of what it was built out of (e.g. stone, brick, or wood), or what kind if objects were used upon the site (e.g. fine ware pottery, glass, coinage, etc). This allows us to consider buildings where we may not have full excavation evidence (and therefore little idea of what the ground plan might be), but it also allows the identification of structures which may not rank highly in architectural terms, but which within their own local context may be more significant than their physical remains would appear to merit. In Chapter Four, for example, it has been argued that the presence of a tile-roofed building in the Fens where there are no villas is more significant than it might be in a comparatively villa-rich landscape.

It is equally important to provide a temporal model (how a landscape evolved over time), as well as a spatial one. It is a danger in studies of archaeological landscapes, where often the dating of evidence is relatively poor, that complex patterns of development over time are collapsed into a crude series of episodes. This results

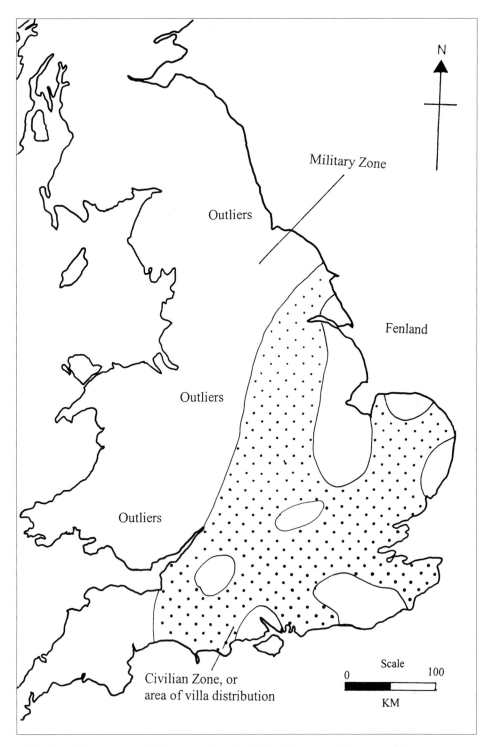

N

Military Zone

Outliers

Fenland

Outliers

Outliers

Scale
0   100

KM

Civilian Zone, or
area of villa distribution

119 Map of the province of Britain showing the division between military and civilian zone.
Note areas within the so called 'villa zone' where no villas are apparent – including the Fens

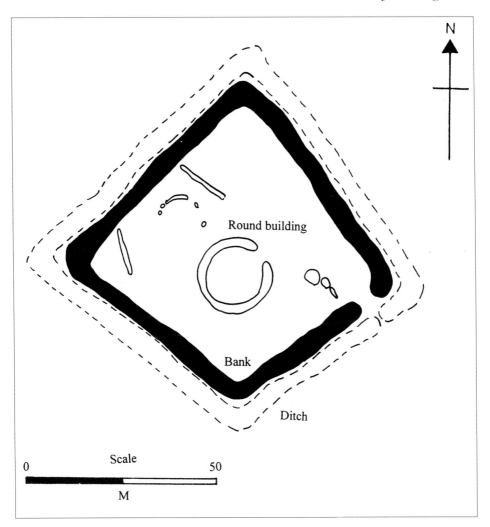

N

Round building

Bank

Ditch

Scale

0   50

M

120 A plan of the pre-Roman/early Roman site of Werrington, near Peterborough. *After Mackreth, 1988*

in a limited vision of the landscape in which consideration is often focused upon the fully developed 'Roman' picture, with little attempt to explore how that stage was reached, or how it came to an end. The evolution of a landscape is continuous and, although limited by the quality of data, an effort is made in this chapter to present a picture of development, i.e. a dynamic model of change over time rather than a series of static pictures. We shall, in effect, attempt to follow the evolution of the landscape from its pre-Roman origins to the end of Roman Britain, to tell the broad 'story' of Durobrivae and its hinterland.

In the late Iron Age, the area that would become the hinterland of the town was divided between two tribes, the Corieltauvi and the Iceni *(121)*. The upland area to the west, the site of the town itself, and the western fringe of the Fens

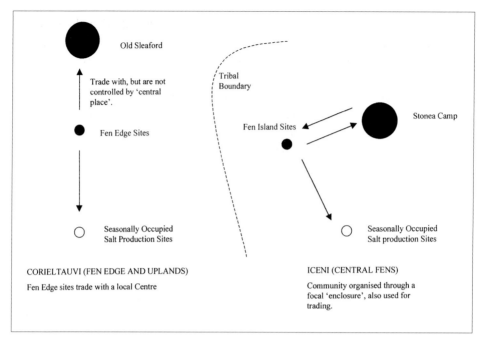

121 An abstract model showing the possible political organisation of the area of Durobrivae's later hinterland in the late pre-Roman Iron Age

belonged to the Corieltauvi. The area of the Silt Fens that would later be a densely occupied area of salt production was, at this time, a vast area of uninhabitable marshland. In the east was the area controlled by the Iceni, the Central Fens with occupation based upon the Fen islands like March and Stonea. We will look at the Corieltauvian areas first.

Salt production was a seasonal activity, and given the evidence for Iron Age salterns in the Silt Fens of Lincolnshire, but the lack of accompanying evidence for permanent occupation, this activity was probably carried out by people living on the Fen Edge moving into the Fens during the summer months. The Lincolnshire saltern sites are located close to this Fen Edge, and the only people with easy access to them were the Corieltauvi – which strongly suggests that they were controlled by that tribe, and this also suggests that the wider demand for salt, or associated products like salted meat, lay to the west. This demand was perhaps focused at Old Sleaford, the site best located to act as a 'gateway' for the Iron Age silts. As already discussed in Chapter Four, the evidence for Old Sleaford is fragmentary; however, it seems likely that it was a relatively sophisticated settlement in the late Iron Age, with evidence for the minting of silver coinage and the importation of goods from the Roman world, like amphorae. The salt and salt meat produced in the Silt Fens may well have been traded here.

Further inland we see a landscape, like much of Iron Age Britain, dominated by individual farmsteads, which may have been the homes of individual families.

Sites like Werrington, Peterborough *(120)*, give us an idea of what these places may have been like, an enclosure, surrounding a round house, set in paddocks and fields, and perhaps connected to neighbouring farms by long drove ways. But there was also iron working, further up the Nene Valley, conducted on a small scale as yet, meeting purely local needs, or perhaps, like the salt production, done by farmers who were exploiting a local resource to supplement their farming activities. There was no settlement on the site of what was to become Durobrivae.

Turning to the area held by the Iceni, there was also an Iron Age population that inhabited the islands of the Central Fens, a community focused around the local centre of Stonea Camp. Iron Age coinage recovered from the camp, a large ditched enclosure on Stonea island, was predominantly Icenian, strongly suggesting that the people of the Central Fens formed a peripheral subgroup of the Iceni tribe located to the east, in East Anglia. Like those living on the western Fen Edge, this Central Fen population also engaged in salt production. Stonea Camp, it has been suggested, might have acted as a trading centre, and wealth generated through salt production may have attracted traders from the heartland of the Icenian Tribe (to the east in modern-day Norfolk). Any wealth generated here would thus have flowed east.

There are two principal features to be recognised in the pre-Roman organisation of the area, then. First, is the east–west division of territory in the Fens between the Icenian and Corieltauvian tribes, though if the interpretation of Stonea Camp as an inland 'commercial centre' is even partially correct it suggests that there may have been a high degree of contact across this boundary. The second feature is that stretching west from the Fen Edge, through what would later become the busy hinterland of a Roman town, was a quite rural landscape of farmsteads.

This area had fallen under Roman control by AD 47, and the early fortress at Longthorpe acted as the major military base in eastern England *(122)*. It was located at the junction between the territories of three tribes, the Iceni, the Catuvellauni, and the Corieltauvi. It was thus placed in an influential location, allowing units based at, or commanded from, this site to maintain a watchful presence on the borders of Icenian territory (still nominally independent as a client state), whilst policing much of the conquered territories of the Corieltauvi and the Catuvellauni. The location of Longthorpe close to the River Nene also suggests that its positioning may have been influenced by a desire to control riverine access to the western areas of Icenian territory, and ultimately access to the sea. Although the Fens lay between the fortress and the Icenian heartlands in Norfolk, the Nene would have been an important means of communication with the Central Fens. By positioning a fortress on the Nene the imperial authorities not only controlled the Corieltauvian and Catuvellaunian population of the vicinity, but could also monitor the eastern edge of Icenian territory. In addition, by controlling the Nene the army would also have controlled contact between the Iceni and the territory of the western uplands, and such a suggestion is supported

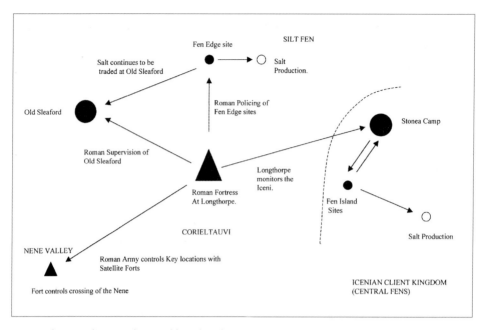

122 A diagram showing the possible political structures in the area of Durobrivae's later hinterland between the years AD 47–60

by the possibility that the western section of the Fen Causeway, the road that the Romans built to cross the Fenlands, may have been constructed in this early pre-Revolt period. This early road, later incorporated into the Fen Causeway proper, would have linked the islands of Whittlesey and Eldernell to the mainland. Longthorpe would thus have acted as an early Roman base from which control was extended eastwards into the Fens.

This pattern of control is also evident in the location of a smaller fort, close to the site of the future town. Its location, close to the river, suggests that the principal function of the fort was to guard the Nene Crossing. The dating of the site is problematic – there have been no excavations. However, it has been pointed out that this particular military site is clearly part of the early Roman fort and road network, and on this basis it is probable that the fort should be assigned to the first years after the occupation. Given the site's proximity, and possibly similar date, to Longthorpe, it is probable that the fort at Water Newton was a satellite of the fortress. Thus Longthorpe and its satellite forts enabled the Roman army to exercise direct control over the Nene Valley, the crossing of the river, and much of the eastern part of the Corieltauvian tribal territory, and some peripheral super-vision of the Central Fens was provided by the fact that this arrangement controlled access up and down the River Nene, perhaps with an early road being constructed eastwards, connecting together some of the closest Fen islands. The Central Fens remained an essentially separate entity from the rest of what was to become Durobrivae's hinterland, belonging to the client state of the Iceni in the east rather than the directly administered territories to the west. By contrast, the rest of the area (part of the conquered Corieltauvian territory) would have been brought under direct Roman control.

It may well have been at this time that the authorities began to take their first interest in the resources of the region. Once the army was established in the area, with several major installations to support, the need to secure key supplies would have been urgent. With the embryonic iron-mining activity to the west of Longthorpe, the works depot attached to the fortress would have become a natural focus for the processing of the metal ore for military use. The fort and works depot might also have acted as a catalyst for later pottery industries, creating a demand for pottery whilst simultaneously creating a production centre that local potteries may have attempted to emulate. This early military presence may also have had an impact upon the local salt-production sites in Lincolnshire, if not yet in the Central Fens, salt being needed to help preserve meat stocks laid down for the military garrison of the area.

Important changes in the organisation of the area appear to have occurred in the mid-first century *(123)*. Although there is no direct evidence, the logical point at which to locate these changes is in the aftermath of the Boudican Revolt, the Revolt providing a context in which to place a drastic intervention by the imperial authorities, and the disruption to local British (essentially still late Iron Age) social structures which appears to have accompanied it. Management of the western part of the area appears to be unchanged, still focused upon the fortress at Longthorpe

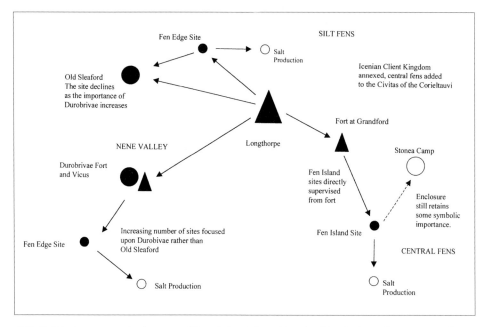

123 Political structures in the area of Durobrivae's later hinterland in the later first century, after the Boudican revolt

and the fort at Water Newton, though both sites were abandoned in the late first century. The timing of these abandonments is unclear, but a smaller fort is known to post-date the Longthorpe Fortress on the same site, and may have continued the administrative functions of the earlier establishment once the bulk of the troops had continued their northward advance. It is also possible that the fort at Water Newton outlasted the main phase of activity at Longthorpe by some years.

Even so, as our evidence suggests that Durobrivae is an essentially Antonine foundation, there remains a gap of several decades between the end of the heavy military presence in the area and the establishment of any recognised civilian administrative structure. Indeed, the traditional view that we have of Britain in this transitional period, that the military moved north and civilian government was established, fails to properly explain how the transition from one form of govern-ment to another occurred. In the case of the area around Durobrivae one option is that, given the presence of valuable resources, official (i.e. military) control continued in limited form. After the area had been pacified following the Boudican Revolt, a military presence composed of small groups of soldiers involved in tax collection and light policing may have been all that was required for continued military control, and continued exploitation of the region's resources. The local elites themselves might have played a significant part in this process, but we shall consider that in the light of developments in the mid-Roman period.

Perhaps the most significant development in the area in the late first century occurred in the Central Fens. As discussed in Chapter Three, it is clear from the kind of pottery used in the Central Fens later on, and from the development of the regional communication network, that by the second century the Central Fens was orientated towards the western Fen Edge and Durobrivae, rather than the *civitas* of the Iceni. How this came about, however, is less than clear. At some early date, probably immediately after the Boudican Revolt, the Fen Causeway was extended east through the Central Fens into East Anglia, and for a short time the fort at Grandford (probably a second satellite of Longthorpe) provided a possible base for the military policing of the March/Stonea area. It is possible that this area was detached from the Iceni in AD 47 following a relatively minor uprising; however, the Grandford Fort, and the road linking the area directly with Longthorpe, only emerge after the later Boudican Revolt. The continued vitality of the pre-Roman centre at Stonea Camp from AD 47–61, evidenced by the large numbers of late Icenian coins which have been recovered from there, and the parallels that we see with another site, that at Fissons Way, Thetford (e.g. both experienced sudden closure in around AD 61), also points to the later date. This makes sense: the oppor-tunity to detach the Central Fens from the Iceni, and reorganise the area on a wholesale basis would have been greatest in the years following the failure of a widespread uprising. One motivation may have been to remove the potentially valuable salt-production industry of the area from the control of a hostile tribe and place it under the same authority as the south Lincolnshire saltern sites, allowing the military to strengthen its control of such a valuable resource in this region.

This, however, still leaves the status of this area in the years following AD 61 unclear. It has been suggested that the Central Fens were directly administered by the military for a period of some years (perhaps about a decade?) after the Revolt. As argued in Chapter Four, this suggests that the local elite were severely weakened at this time. It appears that the army, rather than doing as they had done in more stable areas to the south and planning a single large military installation close to a regional centre of power, had to resort to an approach which gave then closer control – with a fort located near a local centre. This suggests that the Central Fen area was divorced from the wider tribal unit of which it was originally a part, and the closer control the Romans exercised here, as compared to elsewhere, was perhaps a result of the weakening Iceni. The need for the fort at Grandford thus supports the suggestion that the area was removed from Icenian control at this time – having been cut out of a wider tribal structure, the Central Fens required direct military supervision.

After the Grandford Fort was abandoned, we know little about what was occurring in the Central Fens. However, as with the upland, the lack of a fort need not infer that the area had reverted to civilian government. The later construction of the Stonea Tower, and the probable presence of the military at that site suggested by the excavators, may indicate continued official interest in the area. This does not mean that all land remained, or indeed was ever, state property in the manner of a single imperial estate, but does indicate that the degree of control exercised over this area was comparatively close, perhaps because of the salt-production industry and the ability of the Central Fens to produce salted meat for official supply. Between the abandonment of Grandford Fort and the construction of Stonea, it is possible that the area remained under close supervision, maybe in the form of small numbers of soldiers assisting the work of officials. This level of presence would be similar to that suggested by the excavators for the site of the Stonea Tower, though without the purpose-built 'administrative' complex that Stonea was later to provide. Such a phase provides the natural link in the evolution of the area's administration from the military occupation based at Grandford to the construction of the Stonea complex.

Developments in the region in the latter half of the first century AD established the basic structure of the area for the rest of the Roman period, although that structure continued to evolve into the mid-Roman phase, roughly the second and third centuries *(124)*. It has been suggested that following the abandonment of the military bases in this area, an interim administration existed which was comprised of a light military presence supporting Roman officials. These officials will have governed with the co-operation of the native elite who had become involved with the economy of the empire through supplying raw materials for the imperial war machine. This involvement led to the accumulation of wealth by the native nobility, and ultimately the emergence of a villa economy in the Nene Valley, and the town of Durobrivae, which eventually came to support the civil administration of the

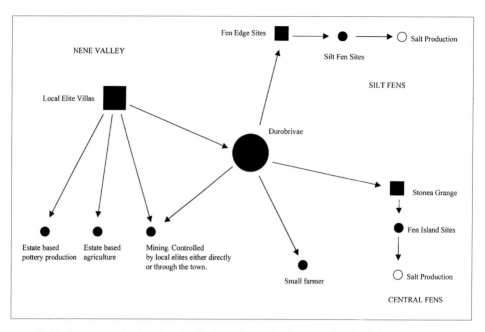

124 Political structures in the hinterland of Durobrivae in the second and third centuries

area. In this scenario the land holdings of the native nobility may initially have been quite small, but growing as the wealth of those who were most successful increased. Essentially, the native nobility seized the opportunities presented to them by the empire, and in doing so they generated considerable wealth for themselves. The combination of a light military presence supporting continued direct administration of the area, alongside co-operative nobles, led to the developed villa economy of the mid- to late Roman period, and the more obvious signs of 'civilian government' following the rise of Durobrivae.

To start we need to dispose of the issue of the legal status of Durobrivae. In the Roman world towns were granted varying levels of status. They may have been, for example, a *civitas* capital or a *colonia*. The curious character of Durobrivae has led some to consider it as a possible *civitas* capital. This is, however, a question unlikely to be settled by archaeology, and, somewhat like our consideration of the problem with defining the villa, we encounter problems when attempting to classify Roman-British towns in a way which revolves around classical legal categories that may not reflect the physical nature of the towns particularly well. The study of Roman small towns is traditionally seen in legal terms (trying to establish what the 'legal' status of a town was). Without evidence that we do not possess, that is a question we cannot settle, so instead we shall concentrate on the archaeology of the town and its surroundings, and consider it in the light of what was actually there.

To examine this process of development of the town in more detail we must begin at the provincial level using a wider model provided by Martin Millett. The province was divided by the Roman authorities into *civitas* territories. A *civitas* was traditionally an administrative area, with a town at its heart. In Britain the Romans used the approximate boundaries of the Iron Age tribes, forming each tribe into a *civitas* with a town, a *civitas* capital at its heart. Millett suggests that small towns, located on the peripheries of *civitas* territories, achieved significant economic growth in the late Roman period (the third and early fourth centuries AD), because they were distanced from these traditional centres of power. Away from the 'dead hand' of the old tribal capitals, individuals were freer to engage in commerce and industrial activity. Thus we see the emergence of these small towns in the border lands as market centres, and we also see the rise of industrial activity, and consequent economic growth, like that seen at Durobrivae. As we have seen, however, the case of Durobrivae is special, made so by its unusually strong links to the army. These links to an area where there was a local elite in the region willing to seize the opportunities that supplying the army offered, and where there were natural resources in the region that the army wanted and territory that could be exploited – i.e. the Fens – underpinned this unusually high level of economic development. However, although extreme in extent, the way in which Durobrivae developed seems to have been consistent with general trends seen at other Roman small towns.

As illustrated in Chapter Two, the evidence for the development of Durobrivae over time is lacking in detail, but a basic sequence for the mid-Roman period has been established. The original *vicus*, a small civilian settlement, grew up around the location of a military establishment at the crossing of the Nene. This then gave way to a ribbon settlement along Ermine Street, with side lanes, and one substantial building, a possible *forum*. At some point a circuit of defences was laid out, though by this point Durobrivae had reached a considerable size, and only the original core was enclosed within the new walls. A section dug through the defences revealed that the bank sealed second-century pottery, suggesting a late second- or third -century date for the walls themselves. Given the broad pattern of development of fortifications around British towns, generally constructed in the second or third centuries, there seems little doubt that those at Durobrivae should be allocated to this period.

Two suburbs, one on either bank of the Nene, grew up along the course of Ermine Street. These would appear to have expanded in the mid- to late second century and to the north of the river at least may have been of a principally industrial nature, though this activity appears to have declined in the third and fourth centuries to be replaced by occupation. These suburbs are important to our understanding of Durobrivae – their expanse is comparable to the area of some of Roman Britain's large towns.

The main element of the economy will have been agriculture. This was probably the case for all small towns, as well as the chief interest of villa owners, and the principal source of their wealth. This is an important point to remember, because there is usually very little direct archaeological evidence for agriculture, as opposed to 'industries' like pottery production. Attempts have been made to reconstruct villa estates, like that at Gatcombe, but these tend to reconstruct villa land as continuous tracts, ignoring the possibility of fragmented holdings, local variation in size of estate, or the processes of 'acquisition and alienation' (the buying and selling of land in an active land market which will tend to lead to the break-up of 'monolithic' holdings). These different factors probably mean that attempting to recreate estates on the basis of the information that we have is pushing the nature of our evidence too far, and this is as true for the Fens and their identification as an imperial estate, as it is for the villas of the west and their wider estate holdings. As with trying to determine the legal status of a Roman town, the archaeological identification of land-holding patterns is a notoriously difficult pursuit, and even a historical approach (looking more at documentary evidence and inscriptions than at the archaeology) is fraught with difficulty, given the anecdotal nature of much of the available data. The certain information that we have for imperial land holding in Britain is very limited indeed, and indirect evidence (salt production, land reclamation and lack of villas, all claimed at some point as evidence that the Fens were an imperial estate) combine only to make this identification possible but never certain.

So landholding patterns were not static, and imperial land, like private land, was constantly being bought and sold, though in general the size of individual holdings seems to have increased over time. This picture of an active land market is based largely upon information from Rome and provinces other than Britain, and we must question to what degree this was true of the area surrounding Durobrivae. The pre-Roman situation in an area often appears to be reflected in Roman-period land-holding patterns, though this influence is not consistent. The location of imperial estates in Asia is predominantly inland, perhaps the same land owned by the crown in the Hellenistic period, but Roman imperial estates appear to avoid areas previously dominated by temple land in Egypt. In Britain we might expect to see the pre-Conquest tribal situation reflected, though perhaps indirectly, in 'Roman' land-holding. If the native leaders in the Fens were weakened after the Boudican Revolt (as argued in Chapter Three), then we might expect to see a high level of imperial land holding in this area, the crushing of the Revolt providing the context for the acquisition of land. However, this does not mean that land in the area remained in imperial ownership – evidence of an active land market makes this unlikely, nor does it suggest that all land in the area was held by the Roman state, or that there was no private ownership in the area at all. Instead we might envisage a situation of mixed ownership, with land owned by the local population, some owned by members of the regional elite, and some (perhaps a higher proportion than elsewhere due to land seizures after the Boudican Revolt) by the authorities. The need to administer this concentration of imperial properties, as well as the value of the local production of salt and salted meat in the Fens and the production of iron in the Nene Valley, may explain the high degree of interest shown by the authorities in this area.

If vast imperial land-holdings were not the main factor in organising the area around Durobrivae, how did the industries function, and what was their relationship to the town? The suggestion followed here is that the whole region, both Fens and Nene Valley, formed the economic hinterland of Durobrivae, and it can only be understood in the context of its relationship with the town. In the Nene Valley large villas are well known, and were clearly the residences of a small group of wealthy individuals. All known villa sites in the country were collected and published in the form of a gazetteer by E. Scott. What this gazetteer reveals is the concentration of sites at Ailsworth and Castor – close to Durobrivae, and up the Nene Valley to the west. Although dating evidence for villas in this area is often slight, most seem to be no earlier than the later second century, like, for example, the structures at Sacrewell and Helpston. Therefore the late second century is probably a period of villa-growth, following on from the expansion of Durobrivae in the early part of that century. Many of the villas are within a relatively short distance of the town, and it seems probable that they were associated with, and given the fact that the town developed first, dependent upon, its development. This clear relationship with the town makes it likely that the villa owners were generally of the class of people responsible for the running and administration of Durobrivae. Consequently they will also have spent considerable sums of their personal fortunes on the town, erecting or refurbishing public buildings. Such people may also have owned much of the property in the town, increasing their involvement with, and perhaps their control over, activity there.

We now have a good outline of the development of Durobrivae and its hinterland, and as good an idea of local patterns of ownership as is possible. But how do the local industries relate to this picture? Durobrivae was clearly the focus for several major forms of production that developed during this period, most obviously salt production, pottery production, and the mining and smelting of iron ore *(125)*. The links between these industries and Durobrivae can never, of course, be anything other than hypothetical, but the existence of a strong connection is supported by the evidence that we do have. With salt, it was suggested above that Old Sleaford acted as the local focus for production, but the importance of the centre declined in the Roman period. It passed from being a politically and economically important site to being a relatively minor one, by-passed by main Roman roads. This contrasts with Durobrivae, which was of increasing importance throughout the Roman period. The layout of local communications in the Fens reflects this, linking areas of salterns with the upland: the only urban centre that had ready access to all of the salt-production areas (both in Lincolnshire and the Central Fens) was Durobrivae, via King Street or the Fen Causeway. If, as we have argued, the regional villa-owning elite of the Nene Valley controlled Durobrivae, it is probable that they also had some influence over salt production. This influence may have been direct, perhaps holding contracts from the imperial authorities to work the saltern fields and being involved in the running of the industry, or indirectly, through control of the facilities of the town. An alternative

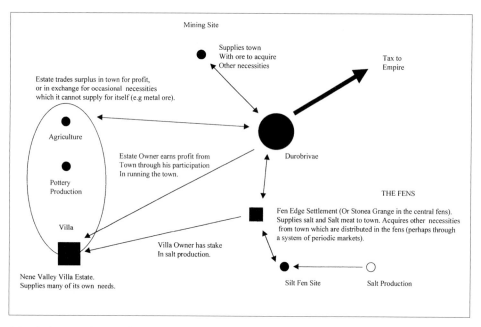

125 A diagram showing how the economy of Durobrivae and its hinterland may have functioned in the second and third centuries, and which illustrates the links between the town and the different parts of the hinterland

arrangement might have been that imperial officials used the town as a base for the continued direct control of local production. This is certainly possible, but what we know of the organisation of Roman industry, even that most closely controlled by the state, suggests that it is less likely than the farming out of responsibility for the day-to-day running of industrial activity on a contract basis.

It was suggested in Chapter Four that the Silt Fens were organised along 'modular' lines with up to five discrete blocks of settlement running different areas of salterns. Each of these communities was linked to a cluster of generally higher-status sites on the Fen Edge, which might each have been responsible for the administration of an area of Silt Fen containing a salt-production community. Each community was provided with a 'status' core, perhaps to provide day-to-day administration. Thus we see a very clear structure in the settlement pattern of the Silt Fens, which allows us to consider the question of market access. As discussed previously, there is a practical limit to the distance people in pre-modern societies will travel to attend a market – usually the distance that can comfortably be walked in one day, say four miles each way, making a round journey of no more than eight miles. When this distance is applied to the Silt Fen communities, we see that it is insufficient for anyone living there even to reach the upland and return in a single day. Access to Durobrivae can thus only have ever been on an occasional basis. Although the actual produce of the Silts may have found its way to Durobrivae, being shipped out by the local elites or the authorities, this still leaves the question of how the natives were supplied with the goods that they could not produce for themselves. One answer, given the distances involved, is a system of travelling nine-day, or *nundinae*, markets, individual communities playing host to the market sequentially. Such markets, attracting itinerants who would be selling on goods available at Durobrivae, would have been an important contact with the outside world.

As well as these developments on the Silt Fen, the tower at Stonea Grange was constructed in the Central Fens at the beginning of this period, after Durobrivae had begun to expand but before the Nene Valley villas had begun to develop. It is unclear whether Stonea represents direct official control of the area, or an attempt by the elite running Durobrivae to control the population of the Central Fens, but these possibilities are not mutually exclusive, and both scenarios may have been played out in different areas of the Fens at the same time, the Roman authorities directly administering some blocks of land, the local elites based in the town running others. As discussed earlier, the construction of the tower may have represented intense official intervention in the area, or (following on from the military government of the area indicated by the locating of the small fort at Grandford) a re-affirmation of external control in a new, perhaps civilian, guise. In either case, the tower probably served as an outpost to supervise the surviving local elite of the Fen islands, as a focal point at which to collect tax contributions, a location to hear legal disputes, and it may also have acted as a base to extend the Durobrivae-based elite's economic interests in the area.

As well as salt production in the nearby Fens, Durobrivae was the natural centre for both the pottery industry and the iron mining of the Nene Valley. The area of villas largely coincides with the area of pottery production and it is thus probable that the same class of individuals who ran the town were involved in the control of this industry. The distribution of Nene Valley ware gives us a clue to how it ties into the economy of the villas and the town – it is distributed across the area identified as the town's hinterland. What this suggests is that, at least to a certain extent, the potters of the Nene Valley had a captive audience in the fellow-tenants of the estates for which they worked. If, for example, the salters of the Fens, or the iron workers to the west, were provided with an occasional market by the estate owner, one way of providing things to be sold at that market, whilst at the same time keeping any money spent within the economy of the estate, would be to sell principally estate products at the market. The salters and the iron workers then, may have been mostly buying pottery produced on the estate. The second element is that of military supply. Connections with the military, forged through the provision of essential raw materials like salt and iron, may well have provided 'informal' opportunities to sell pottery to the army. The pottery of the Nene Valley may have piggy-backed on other forms of trade, accompanying bulk shipments of things like salted meat and iron goods to Hadrian's Wall, and thus receiving subsidised transport – another indication of how army contracts underpinned the local economy.

Mining took place in various locations in the Nene Valley, and more generally across a wider area of the East Midlands, and it is probable that the regional elite would also have had a stake in this activity. At the very least, evidence for the smelting of iron ore in the suburbs of Durobrivae makes it highly probable that ore was brought to the town for reworking into iron items. In addition, the occurrence of small-scale smelting operations near several of the Nene Valley villa sites makes it clear that major sites in Durobrivae's hinterland had access to ore, perhaps via the town. But the organisation of the iron-working sites seems to have broad parallels with the salt-working sites of the Fens, an industry supplying a broad, and certainly more than local demand, probably underpinned by military requirements, and run by local elites in a way that they benefited from the requirements of the military.

We may explore this 'economic sketch' by imagining a hypothetical local landowner, perhaps based at a site like the villa at Sacrewell. We might imagine that this Nene Valley villa owner had a hand in the running of a small number of Nene Valley kilns, located on his land, perhaps like those known from Stibbington and Sibson. Our villa owner would also have been involved with some salt-production sites on the Fens, like those excavated at Helpringham. Perhaps he belonged to a group who held a contract to extract the salt under licence from the imperial authorities – maybe being committed to deliver a certain amount of salt, and/or salt meat to the authorities, any extra produced being profit for the consortium of landowners holding the contract. Our hypothetical landowner's land holdings would not have been concentrated in one block of land, but made up of smallholdings, perhaps both owned and rented, scattered across the region. This 'fragmented' estate would have traded its surplus through the market centre at Durobrivae, or through more local periodic markets, at the same time acquiring the goods to fulfil other requirements that could not be met from its own production. In this model our elite member did not have an involvement in Nene Valley iron mining (not all landowners would have had involvement in all aspects of the regional economy), and so he had to purchase all the iron artefacts that his estate needed from an external source, in this case other estates that did control some iron-working sites, and sold some of what they produced through the town market.

This whole system, of course, was underpinned by the links with the military, forged in the early years of the Conquest. When the army arrived they identified local sources of raw materials under the control of Iron Age chiefs. Under the influence of the military, extraction operations (principally iron and salt) rapidly increased in scale. These were under imperial control, but they operated by being contracted out to people 'on the spot' who could run them, in exchange for a profit. These people may well have been the same class in society as the Iron Age chiefs who had originally run the operation before the Conquest, and so by co-operating with the authorities these people, to an extent, retained their power, wealth, and prestige under Roman rule. When the army moved on, theses sources of raw materials remained tied to the military supply network, produce being moved great distances. It is even possible that supplies went not only north to the wall, but south, and across the sea to the mouth of the Rhine to help supply the legions in the German provinces *(125)*. It has been suggested that Roman officials called *negotiatores* (officials charged with sourcing supplied of the military) based in a place called Colijnsplaat, in the Roman province of Gallia Belgica, traded with eastern England (possibly Romney Marsh, the Kent and Essex coasts, and/or the Fenlands), to acquire supplies, including salt, for the Roman army on the Rhine. This would make Durobrivae a major point of military supply located in a very extensive military supply network, a tradition beginning with the first-century 'military works depot' found near the fortress at Longthorpe. As noted above, this connection is, perhaps, what also underlay the growth of the pottery industry. The link with the military, then, underpinned the large estates of the Durobrivae area, and the unusual concentration of industry that the town supported, and was probably the indirect cause of the rise of the town itself, giving the local elites the money and the opportunity to take over and develop the *vicus* settlement which grew up around the original fort that guarded the Nene Valley Crossing. In short, the military connection, linked to the will of the local elites to co-operate with the empire to make money, explains the unusual nature of the town and its hinterland.

The situation in the fourth century was essentially similar to that in the second and third centuries, but certain features became more exaggerated. The villas of the area had become highly developed by the fourth century, the palatial structure at Castor being a prime example. Other sites show signs of late Roman prosperity, like Great Weldon, with mosaics dating to the second half of the fourth century. The increasing wealth apparent in villas in this area may be evidence of consolidation of land holdings, each villa owner controlling growing estates, a phenomenon noted generally in the Roman world. Even so, the evidence that we have strongly suggests a healthy economy – the presence of a local mosaic school based at Durobrivae from *c.*AD 350, the continued strength of the Nene Valley pottery industry, with a lowered standard of production but relatively wide range of products, and expanded exploitation of iron ore deposits to the west, illustrate this.

What of the rural population itself? Firstly, we might consider the possibility of 'smallholders', individuals running independent farms, perhaps sites like Maxey *(127)*, or Haddon *(128)* selling their produces in the town. The rise of larger estates will initially have been at the expense of these small-holders, something which may have begun in the first century AD, and was presumably an on going process throughout this period, and we might expect their numbers to have declined over time. The progressive consolidation of land holding into larger estates would have reduced the opportunities for independent farming, and living beyond the confines of the great estates, something which, over time would have bound the population closer and closer to those estates. Secondly, those who worked upon these estates may have become tied to their landlords (i.e. to the local/regional elites) as bondsmen in the beginnings of a feudal system. It is

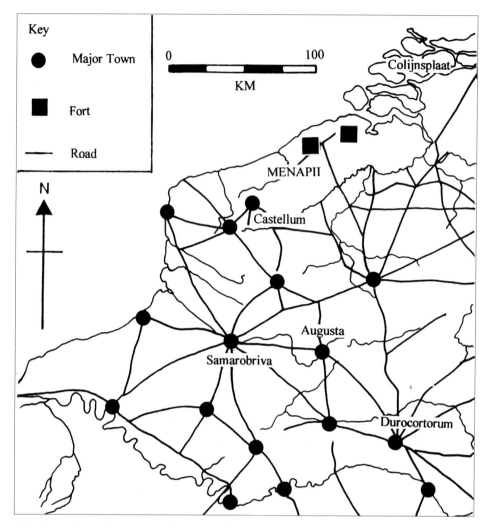

126 General map of western Gallia Belgica. The tribe of the Menapii controlled coastal wetlands, and the region at the mouth of the Rhine, where the settlement of Colijnsplaat acted as the base for Roman officials that gathered supplies for the army. They not only traded locally, but also with eastern England. *After Wightman, 1985. Illustration by Melanie Cameron*

traditionally suggested that this increasing oppression of the peasant class by landowners, combined with various military catastrophes, led to an increasing desertion of the land, and to a decline in agricultural production. *Agri deserti* (as the 'deserted' lands are known) have certainly been considered as a problem in the Fens. But scholars have begun to doubt how significant this problem really was, and it has been suggested that the appearance of this 'motif' of abandonment in the sources had more to do with the early Christian obsession with the end of the world than with late Roman reality. Certainly the increasing opulence of villas in the area, which we have already noted, runs counter to the suggestion that there

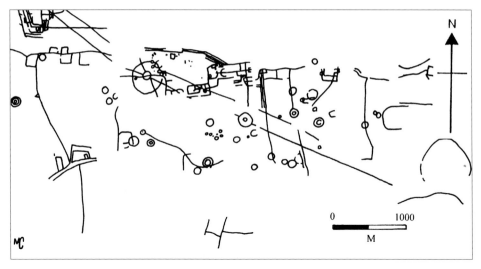

127 Plan of the Welland Valley site of Maxey. This site was interpreted by its excavators as a poor farm with little contact with the outside world, but some contact would have been necessary to pay taxes – possibly at Durobrivae. *Illustration by Melanie Cameron*

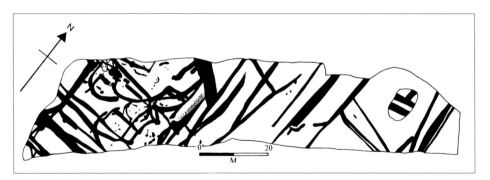

128 Plan of the site of Haddon. Such small farming settlements were typical of the agricultural landscape in the western part of Durobrivae's hinterland. *After French, 1994. Illustration by Melanie Cameron*

was any great crisis in the fourth century. It has even been suggested that a transitional period, dating from 250 to 750, saw a gradual shift from a countryside based upon villas and villages, through a period of 'estates', to a system of parishes and villages. The large, late Roman estates should perhaps be seen as an early phase in the development of what would become the English countryside that we know today, rather than something 'Roman' that was swept away by later events leaving little or no lasting trace.

There are alternative interpretations of this late period on offer. It has been suggested that the peasantry remained largely free, but wealth was concentrated in fewer and fewer hands. The peasantry may have provided labour for the elite in exchange for wages, or on a customary basis, but as the elite turned inward, focusing on private consumption rather than public display (putting their money into building private villas rather than embellishing the town), low-status rural society developed different forms of organisation that resulted in the increasing nucleation of rural settlement, people pulling together into villages rather than spread thinly across the landscape in individual farmsteads. This might have been driven by the decline of smallholding, and the increase in work for wages, villages being pools of labour, whilst the land around them was largely owned by the great estates. This might explain why we see increasing nucleation of settlement on the Fens, at the same time as the increasingly wealthy villas on the upland, though evidence for this late period is notoriously thin, and it is unwise to speculate too far.

In the immediate post-Roman period (say the early fifth century) this situation saw further changes with the collapse of the province. The town of Durobrivae had developed under the control of a local elite based at the edge of the *civitas* territory, and so may have been relatively independent of the 'old' authority at the heart of the *civitas*, based at Leicester. If in the fourth century the provincial economy had indeed become more decentralised, and the *civitas* capitals were exercising less influence than they had in the early Roman period, it is easy to envisage how the collapse of that central authority would lead to the rapid 'balkanisation' of the province (the breaking up of the province into smaller, relatively independent chunks). This opens up a range of possible scenarios *(129)*. If the regional elite survived, we might see most of the regional levels of organisation present in the late Roman period surviving with them. If the regional elite collapsed, then regional forms of organisation that they supported (like, for example, the town council, and big, region-spanning estates) would collapse with them, but smaller units might survive. The evidence of villas in the area around Durobrivae gives some support to a somewhat mixed picture, with much evidence of decline on particular sites like Sacrewell and Bancroft. Though some sites may have begun to decline, the buildings falling into gradual decay, some estates and farms may have continued to function until the end of the fourth century. If the excavator of Orton Hall Farm is correct in interpreting that site as a place that passed intact into Anglo-Saxon hands, a piecemeal process of decline and fragmentation of the 'Roman' social and economic fabric of the area appears the likely situation at this time. Some commentators, talking about the province more generally, suggest that the 'end' of Roman-British villas was a long process of decline running from *c.*AD 350–500, and this must also be the case for the structures of low-status rural society upon which villa economies were ultimately based. Some have even suggested that the 'estate' structure outlasted the villas themselves, perhaps persisting for several centuries.

If models of continuity from the Roman into the Anglo-Saxon period (suggesting gradual change, rather than sudden collapse and calamity) have been

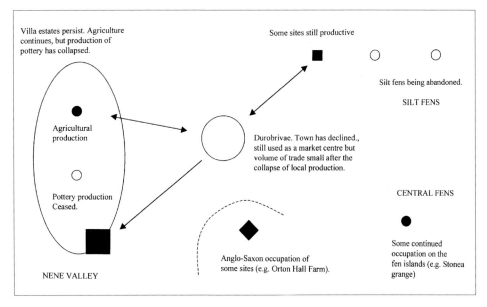

Villa estates persist. Agriculture continues, but production of pottery has collapsed.

Some sites still productive

Silt fens being abandoned.

SILT FENS

Agricultural production

Durobrivae. Town has declined., still used as a market centre but volume of trade small after the collapse of local production.

Pottery production Ceased.

CENTRAL FENS

Anglo-Saxon occupation of some sites (e.g. Orton Hall Farm).

Some continued occupation on the fen islands (e.g. Stonea grange)

NENE VALLEY

129 A diagram illustrating the failing power structures in the region of Durobrivae in the period immediately after the end of Roman Britain

suggested for the countryside in the western part of the town's territory, the situation in the Fens seems to be very different. The Fens, the eastern portion of Durobrivae's territory, were abandoned relatively suddenly. Although it is possible that scattered occupation in the Fens continued for some time into the fifth century, steadily retreating to core areas based upon Fen islands, the vast expanse of the Silt Fens seems to have been largely abandoned by the latest AD 425–450, after a long period of steady decline. With the end of occupation of the Fens, the last vestiges of Roman salt production would have ended also. The end of industrial pottery production has also been seen in more abrupt terms, ceasing by AD 425. Only the exploitation of iron seems to have continued, on a very reduced scale, serving local needs.

This book has been about the town, its economy, and the way in which the whole landscape was organised. But what would it have been like to live in such a place? Of course it is impossible to ever truly enter the mind of an ancient inhabitant of the region, especially given the nature of the evidence that we have to work with, but there are indications. The town of Durobrivae seems to have been an important staging post, and it was certainly the centre of a variety of industries. With much trading, active markets, traffic passing up and down Ermine Street, running right through the defended area at Durobrivae's heart, we get a strong impression of a bustling, lively provincial town, albeit one dominated (like other towns) by the wealthy villa-owning class, who owned houses within the walls, sat upon the town council, and ran many of the local industries. It has been a theme of this book that to understand the town, we must look beyond its immediate and

130 A collection of Anglo-Saxon pottery sherds

narrow confines, and this is certainly true of understanding how people in the area lived. Even within the town itself, we must look beyond the obvious. It may well have seemed a bustling, busy, and relatively luxuriant place to some, but the suburbs show a population living in amongst industrial sites, pottery and iron smelting. For those beyond the walls, making a living from craft, and living close to a pottery kiln or iron furnace, life in Durobrivae may well have been less than pleasant.

Leaving the town, what about the hinterland? Looking east first, we see the Fens. In considering the economic structure of this area, we noted the dependency of the people that lived here upon the industries located in other parts of the hinterland, and upon occasional markets, probably controlled by the estate owner. What does this tell us about the likely life that the salters of the Fens lived? The strong connection with the imperial government and the army seems to have encouraged a sense of tight control over the Fens – not, it must be said, necessarily imposed by the authorities themselves, but by local elites seizing the opportunity to make money from their connections with military supply. The distance of many of the salt-producing communities from major centres of population, far too far for anyone in pre-modern agricultural society to have travelled on any regular basis, must also have increased any sense of isolation from the rest of the region. In short, the inhabitants of the Fens must have lived a rather restrictive and oppressive existence.

What about the people to the west, the agricultural workers, iron workers, and potters? The potters may well have been under closer supervision than other workers in this part of the hinterland. The fact that the kilns appear to cluster in the vicinity of villas mean that the potters were based close to the estate centres, and so may have been working under watchful eyes. Pottery production would have been important to estate owners, not only because it provided a source of income through the connections with the army, but also because supplying pottery produced on your own land to other parts of your estate would have kept the outflow of wealth, caused by importing in things from outside, to a minimum. Iron was also an important resource, and may well have been exploited under imperial contract, a situation which perhaps created similar circumstances to those associated with salt production. The locations where we have identified iron working at the smithing stage (like the suburbs of the town, or close to villas) are often sites where the workers would fall under close control.

Where does this leave us? The ancient world, generally speaking, was not wealthy enough, or developed enough, for large industrial complexes to grow up through the operation of 'market forces'. Although Durobrivae is often held up as an example of such, this is probably a mistake – the town and its surrounding territory do not constitute a general model with relevance to the wider province. Development around Durobrivae was extreme and unusual, so it cannot be held up as 'typical', nor be considered as evidence of a generally developing market economy across Roman Britain. It is unusual, and the real question that we should ask is: what sparked this atypical development? To understand Durobrivae, its industries, and why they developed as they did, we need to acknowledge the long-standing link with the army. The stimulus that allowed growth, then, was the opening of opportunities not available to every town, opportunities that were supported by the 'artificial' (in market economy terms) device of the army-supply network. The money that flowed into Durobrivae came not from the operation of market forces, or real economic growth, but from taxation across the vast agricultural base of the empire. The growth of the industries around Durobrivae, in effect a 'military supply depot' writ large, was the result of the concentration of small amounts of agricultural surplus from a wide area, in fiscal form.

What mechanisms functioned to draw natives into this relationship with the authorities? The impetus initially must have come from the military. This would have occurred at the outset of the Conquest as the legions secured the supplies that

131 Detail of an Anglo-Saxon pottery sherd showing decoration

they required from their immediate locality. This involved, as we have seen, identifying local resources under the control of the local Iron Age chieftains, and ensuring that military requirements were met. In the first instance this may have involved the army assuming direct control of these industries. It might have been the case that the military 'supervised' production, which remained in the hands of chieftains, or even that requirements for resources were presented to local leaders, and there was little interference in the actual mechanics of production, as long as these requirements were met. In any event, it is likely that the initial period after the Conquest, with the army physically present on a large scale, would have been a difficult time for local leaders. Roman demands, particularly on industries still functioning on a small, pre-Roman scale, would have been difficult to meet. It is likely, as industries would have taken time to 'gear up' to meet these higher demands, that military requirements would have to have been prioritised, and any short fall would have been felt by the inhabitants, rather than the army – perhaps leading to shortages of salt and metal objects amongst the local population.

If a harsh, exploitative regime, aimed principally at extracting resources from the area, characterises the early period of Roman rule, how does this situation evolve, and how does this lead to the clear engagement with the authorities by the local elite that we see in later periods? The first development is likely to have been the increasing scale of production in the region. Clearly by the end of the first century, or the beginning of the second, considerable increases in the output of both of these industries had been achieved. There are several possible scenarios to explain this. It may be that the military, having taken control of these resources, systematically set about increasing output, enlarging the scale of operations and perhaps introducing organisational and/or technological changes. If, however, the authorities were simply content to 'supervise' production, overseeing the native elites' efforts to increase output to meet required levels, it is possible that such changes were suggested by the authorities, and enacted by the elites in order to meet their obligations. The final alternative is that, simply in response to a demand for a certain amount of salt and iron, the native elites themselves initiated the process of expansion that was required. If so, it may be that the elites themselves approached the military for assistance.

It is at this point, the point at which industries were expanding and had reached a level where they could supply official requirements, that crucial developments in the relationship between the local elites and the authorities would have occurred. Compulsion on the part of the military to get the locals to supply goods will have only carried developments so far. If we are correct in thinking that it was the local elites that essentially reorganised the landscape to allow more efficient production of, for example, salt, this means that at some point the elites took an active decision to seize the opportunity that the Conquest had offered them. They decided to make the most of the chance to make money from the Roman military machine. What we see, perhaps, in the second century, is an elite that, having in the first century realised that supplying the army would allow them to retain some control over their pre-Conquest sources of income, actually begin to turn the situation to their advantage. If the first century was about surviving the Conquest and its aftermath, the second was about realising that the military had money, working out what it needed, and making sure that activity in and around the town met these needs, but for profit.

This might well be good for the elites – but what about the people who became engaged in these industrial processes? The word 'opportunity' sounds positive, but we should have one eye upon whom the 'opportunity' would have benefited. Whilst the elites were able to finance villas, and some at sites like Grandford (a settlement perhaps with a long history of involvement with the authorities) in the Fens were able to rebuild their houses in stone, most ordinary settlements remained small-scale, relatively poor, and perhaps rather tightly controlled by the estate owners. Involvement in the Roman military supply system does not seem to have brought many appreciable benefits to the ordinary people of the territory of the town – indeed, life working on the salterns, or mining iron ore, with little choice or freedom, struggling to meet not only military require-ments, but also the needs of the estate owner, may have been worse than life in an area which did not engage so heavily with the military supply chain. In short, the army may have created the conditions in which a boom in industry could occur, but the local elites were the ones responsible for wholeheartedly engaging with this opportunity, and transformed the lives of local people, at their own initiative, and in pursuit of wealth. Such a situation did not necessarily benefit the people themselves.

What, then, was Durobrivae? We have looked at the town itself, the connections with the military, the hinterland of the town both in the east, and in the west. It is, as we have seen, a development driven by links with the army, and by the willingness of local elites to seize opportunities to earn money. We often have a view of Roman Britain as a rather standardised place, towns each with the same buildings, forts planned on the same ground plan, roads running straight from place to place. What the unusual extent of development around Durobrivae illustrates is that the way a town in Roman Britain evolved was dependent upon its particular circumstances. Perhaps an important lesson to learn from looking at Durobrivae is that towns in the province were each different, with a different background and history, different economies and probably different politics. Durobrivae was certainly not a typical Roman town, but there was, perhaps, no such thing, and each deserves study as an entity in its own right.

9

TAKING YOUR INTEREST FURTHER

A large amount has been written about Roman Britain and its towns in general, but also about Durobrivae and its hinterland in particular. Below are a few suggestions, outlining the main areas of interest that you might like to read, if you want know more about anything covered in this book.

In Chapter One we looked at the different sources of information available when studying a town, and for Durobrivae in particular. There are some good general books available on archaeological practice, but *The Amateur Archaeologist* (1992) by Stephen Wass is a good starting point, as is *Archaeology: An Introduction*, by Kevin Green. For those that want to know more, *Techniques of Archaeological Excavation* (1993) by Philip Baker is also useful. Much of the information that we have looked at to help us understand Durobrivae is not excavation but has been generated through the techniques of 'landscape archaeology'. Important aspects of this way of studying the past are explored in Michael Aston's *Interpreting the Landscape* (1985), and some of the more technical aspects are looked at in *Seeing Beneath the Soil* (1996), by Anthony Clark. A good way of pursuing this interest is to contact your local museum or historical and archaeological society – they will have details of local fieldwalking activities in your area, which is a good way of becoming involved in archaeology yourself. Those with a more specific interest in ancient maps should consult O.A.W. Dilke's *Greek and Roman Maps* (1985).

If you are more interested in the history of the province of Britannia then the following books would be good introductions: *Britannia* (1987) by S.S. Frere and *Roman Britain* (1982) by Peter Salway. There has also been much written about towns of the period, like *Roman Towns in Britain* (1992) by Guy de la Bédoyère, or if you want more detail *The Towns of Roman Britain* (1995) by John Wacher. If you are interested in the wider landscape, *The Landscape of Roman Britain* (1997) by Ken and Petra Dark is a good, comprehensive (but readable) study. For further information on the Roman-British countryside you should try *Rural Settlement in Roman Britain* (1989) by Richard Hingley, or *Roman Villas and the Countryside*

(1993) by Guy de la Bédoyère. For a wider understanding of the economic themes of this book – try Kevin Greene's *The Archaeology of the Roman Economy* (1986). There is also a series of small books published by Shire Archaeology that offer very good introductions to most aspects of Roman Britain, including the industry of the province in *Roman Crafts and Industries* (1982) by Alan McWhirr. For an entertaining and thought-provoking alternative view try Richard Reece's *My Roman Britain* (1988).

In Chapter Two we looked at the evidence for the town itself. Although you will find information about Durobrivae in the books on towns mentioned above, there are more detailed studies in Barry Burnham and John Wacher's *The Small Towns of Roman Britain* (1990), and D. Mackreth's contribution to *Roman Small Towns in Eastern England and Beyond* (1995), edited by A.E. Brown. Specific information on the suburbs of Durobrivae, which as we have seen were our chief source of excavated information about the urban centre, is contained in *Extra-Mural Areas of Romano-British Towns* (1987) by Simon Esmonde Cleary.

In Chapters Three and Four we moved to look at the evidence available in the Fens. The most recent, and comprehensive study available is *Landscapes of Imperialism: Roman and Native Interaction in the East Anglian Fenland* (2002) by Garrick Fincham. However, this study looks at a wealth of information which has also been published. East Anglian Archaeology have produced a series of reports recording the results of years of survey work, collectively called *The Fenland Survey*, all of which are summarised in a single volume *Fenland Survey An Essay in Landscape Persistence* (1994) by David Hall and John Coles. This book presents the history of the entire Fenland landscape from prehistoric times, although the specific volumes, like *The Fenland Project Number 2, Fenland Landscapes and Lettlement between Peterborough and March* (1987) by David Hall give impressive detail. Also interesting, although hard to find, is *The Fenland in Roman Times* by C.W. Phillips, a study published in 1970 by the Royal Geographic Society, and containing many detailed maps of the region. There is also one major modern excavation report from the Fens, *Excavations at Stonea, Cambridgeshire* (1997), by Ralph Jackson and Tim Potter, with other, earlier, work having been conducted on the site by T. Malim and published in *Stonea Camp, Wimblington: An Iron Age Fort in the Fens, Interim Report*, by Cambridgeshire County Council Archaeological Field Unit in 1992. There is also earlier work at Grandford by Tim Potter, *A Romano-British Village at Grandford, March, Cambridgeshire* (1981), which is certainly worth a look, and Potter's article (published in 1981 in the main annual journal for work on Roman Britain, *Britannia*) *The Roman Occupation of Central Fenland* gives a good overall picture of that area at the time. Religious practices, and their connection to wetland landscapes, is explored by G. Wait in *Ritual and Religion in Iron Age Britain* (1985).

Those interested in the changing environment of the Fens should look at B.B. Simmons' contribution to *Archaeology and Coastal Change* (1980), and Waller's *The Fenland Project Number 9, Flandrian Environmental Change in Fenland* (1994).

In Chapters Five and Six we moved on to the industries in the region surrounding Durobrivae. The general studies of the Fenland outlined above each contain a good overview of the salt-production industry, but for detail of individual sites consult *Fenland Research Number 7* (1992), specifically an article entitled *The Fenland Project, Norfolk*, by M. Leah. There is also *Lincolnshire Salterns, Excavations at Helpringham, Holbeach St Johns and Bicker Haven* (2001), by Anthony Bell, David Gurney and Hilary Healey. For information on a non-coastal salt-production industry see *Iron Age and Roman Salt Production and the Medieval Town of Droitwich: Excavations at the Old Bowling Green and Friar Street* (1992) by S. Woodiwiss. The products of the Nene Valley pottery industry have been explored in a small publication by Peterborough Museum called *Roman Pottery from the Nene Valley: A Guide* (1980), by M. D. Howe, J.R. Perrin and D.F. Mackreth. The industry has been studied in detail by B. Hartley in *Notes on the Roman Pottery Industry in the Nene Valley, Peterborough Museum Society Occasional Paper Number 2* (1960). For the relevance of the industry nationally the general reader should turn to *Roman Pottery in Britain* (1996) by Paul Tyers. Information on the kilns of the industry can be found in *The Pottery Kilns of Roman Britain* (1984) by Vivien Swann. Finally, there has been little published work on either the mosaic school based at the town in the later period, or the iron-production area of the East Midlands. However, *An Atlas of Roman Britain* (1990) by Barri Jones and David Mattlingy gives distribution maps of sites relevant to both, and offers some discussion.

There is a range of excavated settlements in the area around the town that give us important clues about the Roman period. The most comprehensive is probably *Orton Hall Farm: A Roman and Early Anglo-Saxon Farmstead* (1996), by Don Mackreth. An earlier site is that of Werrington, published as *Excavation of an Iron Age and Roman Enclosure at Werrington, Cambridgeshire* by D. Mackreth (1988) in the journal *Britannia* for that year. There is also Haddon, published in *The Haddon Farmstead and a Prehistoric Landscape at Etton: The Archaeology along the A605 Etton-Haddon bypass* (1994), by C. French, four volumes of *Excavations at Fengate, Peterborough* by Francis Pryor, of which the last volume (1984) is the most useful, and Maxey, the report on which forms part of the volume *The Fenland Project, Number 1, The Welland Valley Volume 1* (1985), edited by Pryor and French. There is the military site at Longthorpe, explored in *The Roman Fortress at Longthorpe*, by S.S. Frere and J.K. St Joseph, published as an article in *Britannia* in 1974. The site's role as a supply depot has also been examined by G.B. Dannell and J.P. Wild in *Longthorpe II, The Military Works' Depot: An Episode in Landscape History* (1987), published as a monograph by the *Britannia* journal. These chapters also considered the villas of the Nene Valley, and although little has been written specifically about them, their locations and all references to published works on them are contained in *A Gazetteer of Roman Villas in Britain* (1993) by Eleanor Scott. There are two excavated sites from the western part of the town's hinterland which are worth looking at in more detail, that of Whitwell, published in 1981 as *The Iron Age and Roman Settlement at Whitwell*, and written by M. Todd, and Empingham, published in 2000 as part of *The Archaeology of Rutland Water* by N. Cooper.

Chapter Seven looked at the end of the Roman period in Britain. Most of the general works outlined above will have sections which discuss the closing years of the occupation. However, there are several good specific volumes on this interesting period, including *The Decline and Fall of Roman Britain* (2004) by Neil Faulkner, and *Britain and the End of the Roman Empire* (2002) by Ken Dark.

Finally, Chapter Eight considered the landscape around Durobrivae as a functioning whole. A good general study on the way in which the social, political and economic histories of the province related to each other is *The Romanization of Britain* (1990) by Martin Millett. The history of the Corieltauvian *civitas*, within which Durobrivae was located, is related in *The Coritani* (1991) by Malcolm Todd, although this is now a somewhat dated work, and the name of the tribe/*civitas* used as the title (Coritani, as opposed to Corieltauvi) is felt to be incorrect, as are the boundaries of the *civitas* (which suggest that the Fens and Durobrivae were part of a neighbouring territory). Despite this, however, it remains a good general study. Lastly, the reader is pointed towards an article by J.P. Wild called *Roman Settlement in the Lower Nene Valley,* published in the *Archaeological Journal* for 1974, which draws together much information upon the town and its immediate surroundings, and considers many issues covered by this current volume. Mention is made of the military supply network based at Colijnsplaat, in the coastal wetlands of the continental province of Gallia Belgica, an area covered in detail by Wightman in *Gallia Belgica* (1985).

INDEX

aerial photography 21, 140
agriculture 138-140, 150, 169-170, 175-178
agri deserti 149, 176
Ailsworth 141, 171
Anglo-Roman pottery 156-157
Anglo-Saxon pottery 152
amphorae 73
Anglo-Saxons 37, 146, 149-150, 156, 178
annonae 143
Antonine Wall 108
Appianus estate 123, 142
Ariconium 119
Artis, Edmund 17, 28, 34, 40, 105

Barton Court Farm 158
Beauport Park, Battle 121
Bedford Purlieus 34, 36
Bodium 119
Boudican Revolt 52, 56, 110, 165, 166, 170
Bradley, Richard 92

Castor 122, 141, 171, 175
Car Dyke 16, 77-81
Catuvellauni 51-52, 163
centurion 65
Chedworth 59
Christians 36, 39-40, 142, 176
civitas 36, 143, 168-169, 178
Coldham Camp 20, 66
colonia 168
Corieltauvi 51-52, 56, 110, 130, 161

Dugdale 43, 93
Durobrivae
   abandonment 37-38, 147-148
   aediles 124
   burial 40-41
   cemeteries 40-41
   decurions 124
   duoviri iuridicundo 124
   economy 34
   end of 146-147
   function 147-148
   estates 124, 125
   forum 34, 169, 129
   fourth century 33-36
   industry 32
   inhumations 35, 40-41
   Iron Age 21
   Kate's Cabin 18, 26, 40
   late town 140-142
   legal status 168
   mansio 42, 33, 129
   Nene Crossing 23, 26, 103, 110
   Normangate Field 18, 26-27, 32-35, 40, 103, 105
   Ordo 124
   River Nene 40
   Roman army 23-25
   second century 25-28, 129-130, 169
   suburbs 28-35, 169
   third century 28-33, 169
   townhouses 125
   vicus 169, 175
   Water Newton treasure, 33-36, 39, 142

If you are interested in purchasing other books published by Tempus,
or in case you have difficulty finding any Tempus books in your local bookshop,
you can also place orders directly through our website

www.tempus-publishing.com